THE LAST CANNIBAL OF MARQUESAS

NUKU HIVA

Translated from French by Caroline BRIAND

Zyla TAHI

TABLE OF CHAPTERS

1 - PROLOGUE

On Sunday October 9, 2011, a German yachtsman Stefan, 40, who was circumnavigating the world in a catamaran with his partner Heike, disappeared in Nuku Hiva, a remote island in the Marquesas Archipelago in the South Pacific Ocean. He had gone hiking in an uninhabited valley with a young Marquesan man he met, Arihano, 28 years old. The latter will return alone from the hike and attack Stefan's companion, who has remained alone on board the catamaran. Heike will escape from her attacker and call the gendarmerie.

When the gendarmerie arrive, Arihano has vanished into the wild and Stefan is nowhere to be found.

A few days later, the gendarmes finally found 5.8 lbs of human remains, dismembered and charred, in the ashes of a goat hunter's fire. DNA analysis confirm that it is indeed Stefan.

The news goes around the world. The German press was first moved and the newspaper Bild headlined: "Cannibalism in the South Seas, German vacationer eaten. The authorities suspect the guide, also a hunter, of having cut up his victim, eaten part of his body and burned the rest with dead animals."

The news spread like wildfire in the English-speaking media in Great Britain, in the United States, in Australia, in New Zealand. English tabloid vows readers with Heike's interview: "How I Escaped the Cannibal killer!" the girlfriend of the butchered and cooked tourist recounts her nightmare."

The news is repeated on all sides. The press in France also repeats the news: "Polynesia: A German tourist disappears, the thesis of cannibalism put forward. His girlfriend testified to having seen him leave last week with a local guide, Arihano, for a visit to the south of the island, in the heart of the territories of the primitive peoples, to attend a traditional goat hunt."

The press in French Polynesia, probably judging that all these journalists from the major countries of the world knew more than the Polynesian journalists about what is happening in Polynesia, ingenuously takes up the information.

The Polynesian population, who only read the local press, is dismayed and angry, especially as the international press accuses the authorities of covering up the truth about the act of cannibalism in order to save tourism in the Marquesas.

While this controversy was unleashed around the world, Arihano, the suspected murderer, remained untraceable. For fifty days, the gendarmes tracked him down. The tracking dog was unable to follow his trail, which was lost in the deep valleys and steep cliffs. The fugitive, a great sportsman built like an athlete, knew better than his pursuers, this land which had been inhabited by his ancestors and which he had roamed since his childhood to hunt wild goats.

Arihano ended up surrendering after fifty days and recounting what happened.

The drama experienced by the German couple has revived the cannibalistic terrors of Westerners, that of the Ogre who will eat children who are not good, that of the big bad Wolf who devours the nice Little Red Riding Hood gone alone in the forest.

This book tells what happened in the head of Arihano the Marquesan murderer.

This book lifts a corner of the veil of the history of Nuku Hiva, this story that is not told to young Marquesans, that of their ancestors who ate their enemies, who ate the children, who ate the sailors stranded on their island.

In Nuku Hiva, the descendants of these proud and bellicose Marquesan anthropophagi now welcome tourists with their warrior haka and their bewitching dances resembling a courtship parade.

And a shiver runs down the spine of Western tourists, who remember their forefathers, their skulls split by a warrior's head-breaker before being eaten by the whole tribe.

2 – THE CANNIBALS OF NUKU HIVA

The existence of the island of Nuku Hiva was not known to Western navigators until April 19, 1791, when an American merchant, Joseph Ingraham, who was looking to sell furs on the Chinese market found the island on his way and landed there. Two months later, a French trader, Étienne Marchand who also wanted to sell his furs in China crossed this island on his way and landed at Ua Pou, a much smaller island but within sight of Nuku Hiva.

Nuku Hiva, the unknown, made a remarkable entry on nautical charts in 1791.

From this last decade of the 18th century and throughout the 19th century, sailors, traders, explorers, adventurers, filibusters, fugitives, missionaries, whale hunters from all over the world were attracted by this isolated island in the middle of the ocean, far from everything, covered by no law, and full of cannibals.

All these visitors from another time have brought back to their homes thousands of stories and myths about Nuku Hiva and its cannibals. Here are some examples that have been known to a wide audience.

In English literature, the stories of the American Herman Melville have marked several generations of readers. Herman Melville was born in Manhattan, New York City. In 1840, at the age of 21, pressed by lack of money and work, he joined an American ship specialising in whaling. The whaler makes the grand tour of South America, via Cape Horn, to go hunting in the Pacific, where large cetaceans are numerous. On July 8, 1842, the whaler called at Nuku Hiva to stock up on water and food. Herman Melville takes the opportunity to desert with a companion. The two fugitives were welcomed by the great tribe of Taipi in the valley of Taipivai. The current village of Taipivai is at the bottom of a large bay which bears the name of "Controller's Bay". Herman Melville stayed on Nuku Hiva for a very short time, as a month later he boarded a passing Australian whaler. This will not prevent him from writing long stories about Nuku Hiva.

From his stay on the whaler Herman Melville draws his famous novel "Moby Dick, the sperm whale", inspired by facts, often mythical, circulated in the community of whalers. This is the story of a huge, ferocious white sperm whale which rams the whalers and sinks them. The captain of the ship is a sailor who Moby Dick ripped off a leg in the past. The story tells of the deadly pursuit between the hunter and the whale. The final struggle will end with the sinking of the whaler in Kiribati, with the only survivor being the narrator clinging to the wreckage of the ship. The myth of Moby Dick has never stopped being adapted for film, television or comics. In children's books, Moby Dick has become, over time, a friendly white whale.

Alongside the great novel "Moby Dick", Herman

Melville published an account, inspired by his short stay in Nuku Hiva. It is titled Typee in English which is the spelling of Taipi in French.

The whaler Dolly stops in Taiohae Bay to restock on water and food after six months spent at sea hunting whales. Tom, the hero of the story, does not support life aboard the whaler and is afraid of never returning to his family in America. He decides to desert with his comrade Toby. Both flee into the inhospitable mountains of the island. They seek to reach the Hapaa tribe which has a reputation for being friendly to refugee sailors. In their escape, they must at all costs avoid falling into the hands of the enemies of the Hapaa, the ferocious cannibals of the Taipi tribe. But surprised! their run ends up in the valley of Taipivai among the Taipi. While expecting to be eaten, they are instead warmly welcomed and assigned to live with the family of Maaheiao and his son Kory-Kory. Toby leaves to get medicine for Tom who has a bad injury, but never returns. Tom finds himself alone with his foster family. He falls in love with Kory-Kory's sister, Faiaohae. This makes him discover the mysteries of the valley and the secret life of the tribe. Horrified, Tom attends, hidden, a cannibalistic human sacrifice and discovers in a hut three embalmed heads including that of a white man. Afraid of being sacrificed and eaten in turn, he escapes with the complicity of Faiaohae and joins a whaler, who has gone in search of him.

The book was very popular at the time of its publication, as it pierced some mysteries of this sulphurous island filled of cannibals. Herman Melville published other works on the South Seas. Through his writings, he shows a lot of empathy for these savages who welcomed him. He shows no sympathy for the missionaries who want to convert them to a new religion, for the looters who take advantage of their ingenuity and for the soldiers who want to submit them by force. He weighs the horrible, cruel and bloody acts of the anthropophagi against the no less horrible, no less cruel and no less bloody acts of the Europeans who came to invade them. He wonders whether these island peoples, who enjoyed a natural and pure joy and a health not tarnished by the dreadful diseases that came from Europe, could be happier with the benefits of civilisation that the newcomers claimed to bring them.

When the Europeans arrived, Nuku Hiva was inhabited by several tribes spread over the different valleys. The tribes were constantly quarrelling and reconciling. Raids against each other were always bloody and cruel, ending with the vanquished eaten by the victor.

The oral tradition said that two brothers were at the origin of the tribes of Nuku Hiva. They had irremediably quarrelled and decided to separate by dividing the island into two territories.

Tei'inuiahako, the eldest, took possession of the western part of the island with the very populated valleys of Hapaa, Taiohae and Hakaui. The descendants of Tei'inuiahako are the Tei'i.

Taipinuiavaku, the youngest, received the eastern part of the island with the valleys of Taipivai, Hooumi and Hatiheu. The descendants of Taipinuiavaku are the Taipi.

Since this legendary dispute between the two brothers, their descendants, the Taipi and the Tei'i, have maintained a hostility reminiscent of the steeple quarrels in the villages of deep France.

Those who did not read English, but spoke French, were struck by the adventures of a French castaway stranded on Nuku Hiva. The adventurer is called Joseph Kabris. He landed on Nuku Hiva in 1798, forty years before Herman Melville. Herman Melville is inspired by the adventures of Joseph Kabris to tell those of Tom and Toby in his novel Typee.

Joseph Kabris was the subject of numerous articles in the European gazettes of the time. A journalist interviewed him shortly before his death. Joseph Kabris spoke bad French. The journalist rewrote and published the account under the title "Historical and true summary of the stay of Joseph Kabris, a native of Bordeaux, in the islands of Mendoça, located in the Pacific Ocean, under the 16th degree of south latitude, around the 240th degree of longitude."

Engaged very young in the French navy, Joseph Kabris had been taken prisoner at the age of 16 by the English. In England, he had been forcibly enrolled in Portsmouth on a whaler bound for the Pacific. The whaler arrived in 1798 off the Marquesas.

Joseph Kabris says that his boat was shipwrecked in front of Nuku Hiva and that he had reached the shore, clinging to debris, in the company of the cook. Whoever comes from afar can tell beautiful lies; Joseph Kabris obviously embroidered certain passages from his nine-year stay on the island. In fact, he had probably deserted the whaler.

Joseph Kabris expected to be eaten, but in the end, he ends up, with his English friend, in the Tei'i tribe of the Meau Valley, one of the six valleys that open to the amphitheatre that is the bay of Taioahe. The two men were received by the great chief Keitanui. Keitanui will appear several times in the history of Nuku Hiva with a variable spelling from one author to another: Keitanui, Keatonui, Kiatonui, Gattanewa, Quaitenouïy...

Marquesan is a spoken language. Its writing did not exist. The visitors transcribed as they could the Marquesan names.

Keitanui treats the castaways with great consideration and protects them from curiosity. "In a instant the dwelling of Quaitenouïy was filled with women who followed one another to look at us on all sides," he writes, "making us turn from right to left; and men who kept pinching our skin to feel us, which, while displeasing to us very much, made us fear that we were destined to be eaten"

Joseph Kabris was accepted and integrated by the tribe. He adopted the customs and habits of the tribe. He adopted its habits and customs. He was tattooed and took a wife according to custom. He had two sons. He learned the Marquesan language. He took part in all the events, be it festivals or battles between tribes on Nuku Hiva or on another island. "After the battle, the prisoners are eaten," he writes, "whose eyes, brains and cheeks seem to them a delicacy." Joseph Kabris assures that he did not eat human flesh, but one can doubt it: "These islanders then fight among themselves at the slightest subject of dispute," he writes, "and slit their throats to eat each other, even between relatives. It was at the time of one of these food shortages that I repudiated my first wife, by whom I had no children, for having, aided by her brothers and sisters, devoured her mother and offered to me a part of her."

The adventure of Joseph Kabris will end in 1804 against his will, "finding myself perfectly happy in these islands, where I would still be," he wrote, "if the Russian captain Krusenstern, who landed in these islands to take refreshments and make some exchanges, had not by main force retained me on board to conduct me to St. Petersburg and present me to the emperor Alexander, who showered me with his benefactions."

Joseph, his body covered with tattoos, was a fairground curiosity. The Russian captain presented him to the emperor as "the chief of a tribe of cannibalistic savages". Joseph impressed all the more as he began to speak in Marquesan. Alexander 1er, delighted with the gift, kept him in his service for a few years as a swimming instructor at the naval school. From Russia, Joseph Kabris returned to France where, to earn a living, he toured the fairgrounds showing off his tattoos, wearing a large feathered hat. He spoke Marquesan. Nobody understood but everyone was impressed. Joseph Kabris spread across France a mythical vision of the cannibalistic savages of the South Seas.

At the same time, Edward Robarts, an English sailor, saw an adventure similar to that of Joseph Kabris. It is traced in letters and a logbook he left to posterity. Edward Robarts deserted, in December 1798, the English whaler on which he was a sailor. He escapes to Tahuata, another island of the Marquesas, where he marries a sister of the great chief Keitanui. He eventually settled in Nuku Hiva. With Joseph Kabris, he serves as pilot and interpreter for the scientific mission of the Russian captain Krusenstern. He writes a memoir on the Marquesan language. Krusenstern says that English and French did not get along at all, although they had a similar adventure under the protection of Chief Keitanui. Edward Robarts left Nuku Hiva as soon as possible in 1806 fearing to be the sacrificial victim of an internal war which broke out within the Keitanui family.

A few years later, the story of love, war and peace of an American captain goes around the world. In October 1813, the 32-gun frigate Essex commanded by American Commodore David Porter called at Nuku Hiva to repair damage and allow its 250 crew to rest. Since 1812, the

Americans were at war with the English on all the oceans of the world. David Porter was bringing back 360 prisoners and five British whalers he had seized while they were hunting in the Galapagos Islands.

David Porter knew the stories circulating about the Pacific Islands. When he arrived on Nuku Hiva he was on his guard because he knew that the tribes could behave aggressively. Upon his arrival, the Taïpi and Tei'i tribes, as usual, were vying for supremacy on the island. David Porter decided to get involved. He lowered his cannons ashore and imposed his own supremacy on the thirty tribes of Nuku Hiva. He gave the advantage to the Tei'i over the Taipi. Chief Keitanui, the one who had welcomed Joseph Kabris, became the great chief of the island.

On October 6, 1813, without instructions from the US government, David Porter took possession of Nuku Hiva on behalf of the United States. He named it Madison. To protect his men ashore, he built a garrison which he called Madisonville and a fort which he called Fort-Madison. The Treaty of Recognition of American Sovereignty was signed by the chiefs of the thirty tribes, sealed in a bottle and buried at the foot of Fort Madison. The treaty was never ratified by the US Congress.

David Porter quickly succumbed to the charms of Nuku Hiva. Keitanui, who had become great chief of all the tribes thanks to the American, gave him his granddaughter Paetini, one of the youngest and prettiest of his daughters and granddaughters. She was 17 years old but looked 25 according to the narrators who passed the story on from port to port. She was tall and remarkably beautiful. She had charmed the victor with her slender and graceful appearance. He found in her a gentle, tender, intelligent and sensitive companion. She herself fell in love with this American captain who showered her with presents. One day, Paetini's blood boiled when she noticed that an English fugitive named Wilson, hidden in a bush, was about to fire a shotgun to assassinate her beloved. She leapt into the bush and, risking her life, turned the gun away as the shot went off. Wilson knocked her down and ran away cursing. David Porter, alerted by the shot, thought his princess dead. She woke up under his kisses and with a few drops of brandy slipped between her lips.

David Porter had a palace built for his princess, a European-style house with doors and windows that closed, which did not exist in traditional huts. Paetini quickly found herself comfortable with Western customs, such as sitting on chairs, eating on a table, sleeping on a bed with a mattress and pillows, and storing her belongings in a wardrobe...

David Porter stayed in Nuku Hiva with Paetini until May 1814. Before leaving and before the assembly of sailors he named her "governor and queen of the Marquesas Islands and of all the tribes" and had her declared taboo by the customary authorities. No one was could anymore attempt to her life or even afford to touch her. He promised to come back.

When David Porter left Nuku Hiva, the English fugitive Wilson sought revenge and stirred up the tribes against the occupiers. The fifteen sailors and some English prisoners whom David Porter had left in the Madison garrison were attacked, massacred and eaten by the warriors. Paetini tried to intervene, but could do nothing against popular anger. On May 23, 1814, the bottle was dug up and broken, the treaty torn up and the whole thing thrown into the sea. The garrison was burned. After this carnage, Nuku Hiva regained its tranquillity and independence.

When the navigator Dumont d'Urville passed Nuku Hiva in 1838, fourteen years later, Paetini was still there, beautiful and noble in her palace waiting for the return of her beloved American captain.

3 - NUKU HIVA BEFORE THE EUROPEANS

The Oceanian peoples transmitted their knowledge orally, from generation to generation, from island to island. Nothing was written. Writing arrived with the Europeans. The Marquesans have almost no memory of the stories of their ancestors. The coloniser undertook a profound deculturation to eradicate all ancestral customs, considered satanic, and replace them with a culture based on Christian principles. The coloniser justified his intervention by explaining that he was bringing "civilisation" to these primitive peoples.

The natives of Nuku Hiva were numerous when the Europeans arrived. Quickly, they were victims of a mass extinction, mainly due to the new diseases brought in by the colonists. Syphilis and tuberculosis wreaked havoc on a population that had no immunity to the diseases circulating in the rest of the world.

The Protestant missionary William Crook, who stayed in Nuku Hiva at the end of the 18th century, had counted 6,000 warriors on Nuku Hiva in 1799, which, on the basis of a family of 4, was 24,000 inhabitants. He probably underestimated this population, having no knowledge of the tribes living in distant valleys.

The American captain David Porter who, with his guns and his rifles, had extended his authority to the thirty tribes of Nuku Hiva numbered 19,200 warriors in 1813, giving a estimated global population of 70,000 to 80,000 natives.

In 1853, forty years later, the French military commander of Nuku Hiva counted only 3,150 inhabitants on the island.

In 1866, the Catholic bishop René Dordillon only found 1,000. This number remained unchanged during the count made 10 years later, in 1875, by the French administrator of Nuku Hiva.

The Marquesans, who survived this mass extinction, were banned from tattooing, dancing and carrying on their customs. In schools, children were punished if caught talking in Marquesan. Masks, statues and customary artefacts were broken, burned. The collective memory has been erased.

Before everything disappeared, a few Westerners took notes on the habits and customs of the Marquesan natives.

The Catholic bishop René Dordillon, who arrived in Nuku Hiva in 1845, wrote a "Grammar and Dictionary of the language of the Marquesas Islands ". The bishop was aware of the imminent extinction of the Marquesans because, in the presentation of the work, he emphasises: "As this people becomes extinct, ethnographers and linguists will appreciate more the documents written in a language which will no longer be spoken."

Sculptures, everyday utensils, ornaments, masks, totems, pirogues were taken away by visitors, settlers, soldiers, missionaries and looters. All these memories are scattered around the world, in attics, in private collections or in museums. At the "Musée du Quai Branly", in Paris, known as the "Musée des Arts Premiers", the Marquesans can see objects that belonged to their ancestors. They no longer find such memories of their past on their own island. The destruction of memory was such that in 2022, the Parisian museum loaned artefacts looted in Polynesia during the colonisation period to the Museum of the Islands of Tahiti, so that Polynesians would have knowledge other than books of their past. In this loan, there are some artefacts stolen from the Marquesas, in particular, the feathered headdress of the great chief Pakoko, descendant of Keitanui, this great chief who had welcomed Joseph Kabris and Edwards Robarts and who had become great king of Nuku Hiva thanks to the cannons of David Porter. Pakoko had been shot in 1845 by French soldiers following the massacre of a few sailors who had not respected a taboo.

In the list of Westerners who have worked positively to preserve the memory of the past of Nuku Hiva, the German psychiatrist Dr Karl von den Steinen holds a good place. He stayed six months, in 1897 – 1898, on Nuku Hiva. He was passionate about these people. "Almost too late", he wrote. He learned Marquesan, travelled the valleys and recorded the stories. He noted all the tattoos with their context and meaning. Because of the First World War, he could not publish his work until 1925. He published an three-volume encyclopaedia, very rich in iconography of tattoos.

When the Marquesans, from the 1980s, began to lift the religious screed that masked ancestral customs, they found in the encyclopaedia of Dr. Karl von den Steinen the tattoos of their ancestors and their meaning.

To go back even further in the history of the Marquesans, we must call on archaeologists, linguists, ethnologists, historians, prehistorians and many other scientists...

Genetics as well as the analysis of linguistic evolution and customary practices bring the origin of the peoples who colonised the Marquesas Islands to a people from south-east China and especially from Taiwan, who, 6,000 to 7,000 years ago, knew how to fish with outrigger pirogues, make fabrics by beating bark and bake clay to make utilitarian objects. These primitive people cultivated some plants and trees useful for their survival.

Groups from this Asian people will migrate to Papua New Guinea and occupy the geographical area of Melanesia. It is from the Solomon Islands, in Melanesia, that a new migration will appear, 3,000 at 3,500 years back, which will progress, towards the east, from island to island, throughout the South Pacific. These migrants managed to reach distant and uninhabited islands and to settle there because they mastered new techniques of navigation and new knowledge in agriculture and animal husbandry. They also mastered the manufacture of terracotta pottery.

In scientific journals, they are called Lapita, from the name of the archaeological site in New Caledonia where a geologist found, in 1956, pottery of a craftsmanship that archaeologists did not know. These are pots, dishes or jugs, decorated with complex geometric figures and sometimes stylised human figures.

The Lapita were good navigators. They were able to colonise islands located several hundred miles away in the open ocean thanks to the invention of outrigger pirogues. These prehistoric boats could transport families, domestic animals and food supplies. Large outrigger pirogues, on which a shelter was built, were still in use in the 19th century in the Solomons and allowed families to travel, without difficulty, to distant islands, such as Samoa, further east. The Lapita were able to orient themselves on the ocean and they maintained relations with their congeners on other islands.

The Lapita, for food, cultivated plants such as taro, yams, bananas and coconuts which became the staple food of all the islands of the Pacific. They raised, for their consumption, small animals, like the dog, the hen and the pig. Their diet was supplemented by seafood, for those who lived on the coast. The Lapita are the ancestors of the Polynesians. They spoke an Austronesian language from which the Polynesian language and all its dialects were born. Austronesian is a family of languages whose domain extends from Taiwan in the North, to New Zealand in the South and from Madagascar in the West to Easter Island in the East.

The Lapita emerged from an area of the Pacific already occupied for 40,000 to 60,000 years by migrants who had taken advantage of the drop in sea level to reach Australia and Papua New Guinea, which had formed one big continent. However, Polynesians are genetically unrelated to Australian Aborigines of Australia and New Guinea Papuans.

The Lapita successively occupied the islands of the South Pacific from west to east, leaving a trace of pottery bearing characteristic geometric decorations. The Lapita arrived in the Marquesas a little over 3,000 years ago, as evidenced by the oldest pottery found there.

The Lapita who have progressed the most easterly of the South Pacific will gradually transform into

Polynesians. The first characteristic elements of Polynesian culture appeared 2,500 years ago, while the Lapita culture was fading. The most recent Lapita pottery is 2,300 years old. By becoming Polynesians on islands rich in marine resources, easy to collect and consume, the Lapita forgot the technique of making pottery, which they no longer needed. They gave up their farming heritage, since there was no longer any need to farm to survive. The elaborate utilitarian artefacts they needed in everyday life were made from wood, stone, bone or turtle shell.

Polynesian culture is characterised, first of all, by its language, Polynesian, which belongs to the large family of Austronesian languages. On each island, the islanders speak a dialectical variant that is easily understood on neighbouring islands. This linguistic community maintains a unitary cosmogony. The vision of the organisation of the universe is common to all Polynesians. The earth is considered as a marine living being in a universally oceanic space. There is a creator god and sub-divinities who live in a supernatural world, set in the darkness of night. Living things have a supernatural afterlife and can come to haunt the living. The divine beliefs of the Polynesians are quite difficult to reconstruct in their most primitive forms, because the narrative was very quickly contaminated by the beliefs of the Europeans.

Taboo and mana are two concepts specific to Polynesian culture. The taboo is a prohibition, dictated by the god or gods, pronounced by the chief of the tribe or the high priest. The violation of a taboo is punishable by death.

Mana is the vital principle that animates all beings, whether human, animal, vegetable or mineral. Mana gives strength and power. The mana of each being is related to the universal mana. For a human being, the connection of his own mana with the supernatural mana is on the head. The Polynesians manifest this by making, with their hair left long, a very high bun on the top of their head. On the monumental statues, or moai, of Easter Island, mana is symbolised by the pukao, the red stone headdress placed on the head of these huge statues. By eating his vanquished enemy, the Polynesian warrior believed he was acquiring his opponent's mana.

Polynesian culture has settled in the Polynesian Triangle, a geographical triangle of the South Pacific pointed by Hawaii to the north, Easter Island to the east and New Zealand to the south. Within this triangle are Samoa, Fiji, Tonga, Cook, the Marquesas and Tahiti.

The Polynesian people were able to reach South America. The sweet potato is an index of the stay of the Polynesians in South America, from where they would have brought the sweet potato, because this vegetable, which is today largely cultivated in the South Pacific, is native to this continent. The oldest sweet potato fragments have been found in the Cook Islands. They are 1,000 years old.

Other scientists think that it was the Amerindians who were able to come to meet the Polynesians. This is what the Norwegian Thor Heyerdahl wanted to demonstrate with the Kon-Tiki expedition in 1947. The Kon-Tiki is a raft built using technology used in the powerful Inca kingdom, a kingdom that disappeared completely after its destruction by the Spanish conquistadors. Leaving Peru, the Kon-Tiki, carried by sea currents and helped by a rudimentary sail, ended up reaching the Polynesian atolls of the Tuamotu archipelago.

The Polynesians invested or reinvested islands that

had previously been discovered by their ancestors the Lapita. Like the Lapita before them, they reoccupied the Polynesian triangle by advancing from west to east. Over the centuries and the constant movement of pirogues on the ocean, the Polynesians have perfected their knowledge of astronomy, geography and navigation.

The Polynesians used veils made of braided pandanus leaves or tapa sails, this fabric made from the long-beaten tree bark. They had learned to ride the wind. The trade winds in the South Pacific blow steadily from east to west, making it easy to return to the starting point when the pirogues explored the easternmost islands.

The Polynesians orientated themselves in the ocean thanks to the paths of the stars, traced by the gods in the sky. They had conceptualised the sky as a navigation tool. It was their GPS, their global positioning system. On several occasions during their exploration, Westerners took Polynesians on board their ships to pilot them across the Pacific. Even when they had never been there, Polynesian pilots knew how to reach a distant island by following the path of stars that led there. They were able to bring western ships from the Marquesas to Hawaii, 2,300 miles north, or from the Marquesas to Tahiti, 900 miles south, or to New Zealand, 3,500 miles even further south. These paths known from time immemorial were transmitted to subsequent generations by oral tradition. Thus, the collective memory of the Polynesians concealed an enormous mass of information which unfortunately was not written down when the Europeans arrived with writing. The memory has been erased, replaced by the European method of orientation, with the compass and the sextant.

The Marquesas were reached from the islands of Samoa and Tonga using large double hulled pirogues, equipped with sails. The first westerners who arrived in the Polynesian triangle saw double pirogues up to 60 feet in length and carrying up to 80 passengers. The double hulled pirogues were made of sewn planks and the veils of braided pandanus leaves.

It was from the Marquesas that the large migratory double pirogues left that populated the islands at the ends of the Polynesian triangle, Hawaii to the north, Easter Island to the east and New Zealand to the south.

Although scattered on islands out of sight, the Polynesians always remained in contact with each other. Marquesans continued to travel to the islands which their ancestors had departed, Samoa and Tonga, 1,800 miles and 2,500 miles respectively to the west. The inter-island relational network has always been very active, maintained by incessant comings and goings of large double pirogues for long journeys and small sailing and rowing outrigger pirogue for short distances.

The arrival of large western vessels, military frigates, merchant ships, whalers, caused the decline of the large pirogues and their complete disappearance in the middle of the 19th century.

The first Polynesian groups who arrived in the Marquesas, 2,500 years ago, settled on the coastal edges of the islands and adapted to their new environment. Although they brought in their luggage some food plants and some animals for their consumption, they did not seek to develop agriculture and animal husbandry. Marine resources were varied, abundant and easily accessible. They provided most of the food as well as the necessary protein supply. This ease of feeding is probably one of the reasons why the Polynesians have forgotten the know-how in agriculture, animal husbandry and pottery making of their Lapita ancestors.

In their various dialectal language, the Polynesians define themselves as the Maohi, Maori, Mao'i people... literally, the people of those "who gather their food".

The first Marquesans harvested shellfish and gathered crustaceans. In shallow water, at the edge of the shore, they captured fish with a harpoon, a spear fitted with a point made of hard wood, bone or mother-of-pearl.

The fisherman stabbed the fish that approached or threw his harpoon to pierce the one that passed from a distance. The Marquesans, over the generations, have acquired a great knowledge of the marine species that constituted their food resource. They had recorded the biological rhythms, the migratory passages, the influence of the lunar cycles...

Between the first settlement of the Polynesians in the Marquesas, 2,500 years ago, and the arrival of the first Westerners, 400 years ago, a period of 2,100 years passed which can be roughly divided into three periods: an first period of 500 years of coastal occupation, followed by a second period of 1,000 years marked by demographic grow, leading to the increasingly important occupation of the vallcys away from the coast and to a modification of the food resources, and finally, a period of 600 years where the demographic saturation of the island leads to an significant modification of the social organisation and to an intense practice of anthropophagy as a means of demographic regulation.

The first five hundred years of occupation of the islands, there was room for all the Marquesans on the edge of the ocean and resources were abundant. The Marquesans did not seek to develop their technical knowledge. It was the era of every man for himself, where everyone collected what he wanted where he wanted, outside of any constraint imposed by a chief or any authority.

In the following millennium, i.e., in the first millennium of the Christian era of Westerners, the Marquesan population had increased to the point of creating competition for the collection of seafood products along the coast. The Marquesans have started to plant, here and there in the hinterland, species providing food supplements such as coconut, banana and breadfruit. These were not organised plantations. The Marquesans were still hunter-gatherers. By promoting the growth of fruit trees in the forest of the valleys, they increased their chances of picking. The breadfruit tree, once planted, does not need to be maintained. It provides edible fruits all year round which can reach six to nine pounds. The fruit needs to be cooked to make it digestible, but cooking is fairly simple. You have to cook the fruit to make it digestible, but the cooking is quite simple. In the embers of a fire, its outer shell chars and the inner flesh becomes tender and tasty. Westerners compared the cooked fruit to bread with its crust and crumb. This is why the tree kept this name of breadfruit tree. The breadfruit, during this millennium, became an increasingly preponderant part of the daily diet of the Marquesans.

The Marquesans who had lost the use of the pottery used by their Lapita ancestors developed an original technique for preserving food in particular the breadfruit. They peeled and cut the fruits, piled them up in a stone pit lined with leaves, covered them with leaves, then closed the pit with stones which by their weight compressed the preparation. The fermentation of the fruits caused the stones of the lid to collapse and indicated the end of the fermentation. At the opening appeared a pasty fermented mixture, the popoi in

Marquesan. It kept for a long time and the Marquesans drew it according to their needs. It made it possible to deal with periods of scarcity caused by climatic hazards, such as cyclones or droughts. The technique of storage progressed over the ages. The pits became bigger and bigger and the amount of pulp stored bigger and bigger. The fermentation technique has improved giving the popoi longer and longer shelf lives, up to several years.

During the six hundred years preceding, in 1595, the arrival of the first European in the Marquesas, Alvaro Mendaña, the Marquesan population grew so much that all the habitable spaces of Nuku Hiva were occupied. This is the period of population saturation in relation to available food resources.

The island of Nuku Hiva is the emergence above the surface of the ocean of a gigantic underwater volcano which rests 10,000 feet below on the tectonic plate. Only half of the crater remains of this summit, the Toovii plateau, 2,600 feet above sea level surrounded by a steep semi-circular ridge. The other half of the top of the volcano has disappeared. The whole circumference of the island is just basalt cliffs that plunge deep into the ocean. The volcano has been extinct for two million years. Erosion has cut into this huge block of lava and caused deep valleys that open up to the sea, forming bays. The best known valleys and bays are Taiohae and Taipivai. They concentrate most of the island's population and offer the most accessible anchorages for western boats.

Much of the island is uninhabitable as there are only steep peaks and rocks where vegetation fails to sustain itself. On the other hand, at the bottom of the valleys, men found forests, edible plants and streams that provided fresh water, vital to life

When all the valleys were occupied in all their nooks and crannies, access to food became difficult, very competitive between the various inhabitants and very uncertain due to natural disasters, droughts, cyclones, sometimes tsunamis and can-be epidemics. Dietary stress has induced radical social changes.

Marquesans grouped themselves into hierarchical tribes with warrior castes and omnipotent chiefs, to defend the living space of the community and its food resources. As access to the sea became more difficult, valley bottom tribes developed food crops and traded their agricultural products for seafood with the coastal tribes.

Community spirit has grown. Each member of the tribe occupied a defined social role and benefited in return from the food collected or produced by the community. This social organisation and the rules that govern it are commonly called custom.

Community mutual aid allowed tribes to increase food resources by carrying out agricultural production on a larger scale.

Under the direction of the chief, the tribe dug in the ground imposing stone silos to preserve the popoi. It was the survival food stock to deal with the unexpected. These pits were a stake in wars between tribes, as the destruction of the tribe's food stock threatened its survival. The community pits were therefore hidden. It happens, nowadays, that one finds inviolate pits which contain their precious fermented dough, still edible, it seems.

The community spirit made it possible to develop the culture of the taro, because the construction and the management of a taro field became possible with the help of the members of the tribe. The taro bed is a basin with a raised edge that retains rainwater in which we plant taro, a tropical plant that requires very humid soil. Its tuberous root is edible but like the potato, it must be cooked to make it digestible. Taro became, during this period, the staple food of the Marquesans.

In coastal areas, the need for more elaborate fishing methods to feed an ever-growing population has led to the emergence of sophisticated fishing techniques for catching big offshore fish. The Marquesans made hooks, made of bone or mother-of-pearl, attached to the end of twisted vegetable fibre lines, which were very robust and caught the tuna in depth.

The tribal structure has done away with the notion of each for himself in favour of each for all. The individual fades into the body of the tribe of which he is no more than a link. He owns nothing, everything belongs to the tribe, even his biological children who are raised by others than him. If he brings back food, he shares it with his tribe and keeps only the share that custom grants him. He decides nothing, all his actions and behaviours are regulated by custom. The tribe has the right to life and death over him and his family without him feeling any injustice. He does not object to his biological child being sacrificed and eaten, if such is the will of the tribe, and he himself eats his share.

Tribal authority is embodied by the tribal chief who organises social life according to custom and by the high priest or high priestess who invoke the gods or interpret their wishes. Tribal authority is enacted in the form of a taboo. The taboo is an inviolable prohibition, pronounced by the chief or the high priest. Violation of a taboo results in immediate death.

The tribe is stratified into upper and lower castes. Warriors occupy a superior social position. They are the first eaten by the victor, during tribal wars, because they have the most powerful mana.

The role of women is very clearly defined. As the children do not belong to his progenitors but to the tribe, it matters little who the progenitor is. Even if a woman and a man form a couple, it is considered normal for the wife to have a child with another man.

The position and social role of each member of the tribe are fixed by increasingly strict and complex customary rules over the generations, locked by taboos, enacted by despotic tribal chiefs.

Survivals of tribal behaviour persisted well into the 20th century. Polynesian social behaviour in the 21st century is in rapid extinction starting with Generation Z who grew up with social networks. Young Polynesians align themselves, today, with social representations globalised by social networks rather than with the behaviour of their parents.

The strangest tribal survival in terms of Western practices concerns the child's belonging to the clan rather than to its parent family. It is the fa'amu child, that is to say a child raised by a family that is not its biological family. The child is voluntarily handed over by his or her parents to the new family, where he or she acquires the same rights as biological children when they have not themselves been entrusted to another family.

Despite the rigour of the Christian religion on the respect of fidelity within the couple, Polynesians, women and men, have long continued to unite in a plural way without anyone finding fault. The many children of the same family come from several different fathers, so much so that we never use the married name in administrative relations, but the maiden name.

Despite the establishment of Western democracy

based on a balance between power and counter-powers, the unquestionable authority of the tribal chief was transferred in the 20th century to the authority of the President of Polynesia or, failing that, to the authority of the mayor of the municipality. The chief decides on everything and everyone accepts the chief's decision without criticism and without question. The behaviour of the latter is never questioned, even if he is prosecuted for having embezzled the funds of his constituents. He is the chief; he has all the rights. A few crooked chiefs during the colonial period took advantage of the blind allegiance of their subjects to sell tribal lands claiming to be the sole owners.

The tribes lived under permanent food stress, linked to the reduction of living space, caused by demographic saturation and climatic hazards. Famines were repetitive and resulted in large number of deaths. Each tribe sought to gain an advantage over the neighbouring tribe. By eating the warriors of the defeated tribe, the victorious tribe found the protein supply that the sea no longer provided.

When the Europeans arrived in Nuku Hiva, the inhabitants were in a demographic stalemate. The island could not provide enough food for everyone. The surplus population could not migrate to another island because all the islands of the Pacific, even the most inhospitable ones, were already occupied and faced the same problem of demographic saturation. The demographic balance was maintained by intertribal killings and anthropophagic practices.

In two thousand years of evolution, the Marquesans, thanks to technological advances in agriculture and fishing and a more cooperative social organisation, had managed to cope with their population growth. in the year 1600 of the Christian era, when the Westerners arrived, they were at the end of the reception capacities of the islands and had no prospect of new technological advances which would have allowed the population to continue to grow.

4 - THE COLONISATION OF NUKU HIVA

The Spanish admiral Alvaro Mendaña de Neira was the first European discoverer of the Marquesas. It was at the end of the 16th century. He had left Peru with 4 ships. Peru had become a colony of the Catholic kingdom of Spain, governed by a viceroy, after the ancient kingdom of the Incas had been savagely conquered forty years earlier by a Spanish soldiery thirsty for gold, the conquistadors. Alvaro Mendaña's expedition was officially on a mission to convert the pagans to Christianity, but it was only an honourable cover that hid an unbridled thirst to grab new wealth.

Alvaro Mendaña knew the Solomon Islands which he had discovered twenty-eight years earlier. He had given them a name taken from the Bible, that of King Solomon. The name has remained until today. It was there that Alvaro Mendaña, and with him the Westerners, discovered Oceanian cannibalism when the islanders offered him a quarter of a boy to eat with his arm and hand.

On the way to the Solomons Alvaro Mendaña saw on

July 21, 1595, a group of unknown islands. These were the islands which bear the present name of Tahuata, Fatu Hiva and Hiva Oa, and which are grouped to the southeast of the Marquesas.

Access to the shore of Tahuata seeming difficult to him, Alvaro Mendaña continued to Fatu Hiva. He saw arriving to meet him more than four hundred islanders in a multitude of pirogues. He sent a boat to reconnoitre the place. As soon as the sailors set foot on the shore, they were greeted, to their surprise, by a swarm of women who did everything to seduce them. The men then arrived, but the exchanges remained friendly and respectful. Faced with this warm welcome, Alvaro Mendaña said himself that he was probably not the first European to visit this island.

The inhabitants of these islands may have heard of these navigators who came from afar on large boats. Since time immemorial, Polynesians have maintained inter-island relations throughout the Pacific. The story of Alvaro Mendaña's passage to the Solomon Islands, twenty-eight years earlier, had had time to spread from one end of the Pacific to the other, more than three thousand miles.

Gradually, the natives, boarding the Spanish boats, grew bolder and began to pilfer all they could. They were very interested in metal artefacts. They did not know iron. They were fascinated by nails. With nails they could make tools or weapons far more effective than those they made with bones or tortoiseshells. The men tried to pull out the nails, wherever they found them, while the women held the attention of the sailors.

Fearing the worst for his ships, Alvaro Mendaña had the guns loaded and fired into the crowd. Eight pilferers, including a chief, were killed. The "savages", frightened, fled and disappeared into the forest. A little later they came back with pigs, coconuts and breadfruit. The natives had no way of imagining what and how iron artefacts, such as nails, swords and guns, were made. The only plausible explanation was that the gods had provided these beings from nowhere with these iron artefacts. The natives therefore had to appease the wrath of these sailors sent from the gods so as not to be overwhelmed with an even more devastating divine wrath.

In Hiva Oa, the encounter between the sailors of Alvaro Mendaña and the natives quickly turned sour and a hundred natives were shot dead.

Alvaro Mendaña took possession of these new lands in the name of the Catholic King of Spain and named them "Las Islas Marquesas Don García Hurtado de Mendoza y Cañete" after the Viceroy of Peru who ordered the expedition. The name has survived under the current name of Archipelago of the Marquesas.

Mendaña did not linger in the Marquesas and his convoy resumed the direction of Salomon. Alvaro Mendaña had not identified Nuku Hiva but it was he who chose the name that is used today to designate the Marquesas archipelago and its inhabitants, the Marquesans.

The Marquesans no longer saw, for 179 years, boats from the West.

The next visitor was a famous English navigator, Captain James Cook, sent by the Royal Society of London to explore the southern seas in search of the Antarctic continent. On the way to the polar circle, he stopped on April 6, 1772 in the islands previously discovered by Alvaro Mendaña. He remained only four days at anchor off the island of Tahuata. Knowing the conflicts with the population that had arisen during the passage of his predecessor, he immediately imposed himself on the Marquesan warriors with noisy but harmless firecrackers. He did not perpetrate massacres among the population.

James Cook was unaware of the existence of Nuku Hiva and the sister islands. They always remained unknown to Westerners. However, the passage of James Cook marked a turning point in the life of the Marquesans, because their islands were now perfectly identified on the maps of the World of Westerner. These distant islands, lost in the middle of the Pacific Ocean, still mysterious, then attracted a multitude of visitors from all over the world and animated by the most diverse intentions. Explorers, scientists, traders, missionaries, megalomaniacs, fugitives, deserters, pirates descended like flies on the Marquesas

If James Cook knew nothing of the existence of Nuku Hiva, the people of Nuku Hiva were quickly informed of his passage to Tahuata by the inter-island network.

James Cook had an end in keeping with the legends of the South Seas. He was killed and eaten by Hawaiian islanders in 1779, seven years after he passed through the Marquesas.

The first Westerner to set foot on Nuku Hiva was an American. His name was Joseph Ingraham. In 1791, nineteen years after the passage of James Cook, the Marquesans of Nuku Hiva saw for the first time a Western ship and Western sailors. Physically the difference between Marquesans and Westerners was not striking. The French captain Etienne Marchand who arrived a few days later in the footsteps of Joseph Ingraham describes them:

"The inhabitants are tall, strong and extremely agile;

the colour of their skin is a light brown but there are many who hardly differ from Europeans of the lower class. They have no clothing other than tattoos, the climate requiring none. These drawings are distributed with the greatest regularity." Etienne Marchand was impressed by the quality of these designs harmoniously distributed over all the body.

Captain Joseph Ingraham was a merchant originally from Boston. Inspired by the tales of James Cook, who had bought furs on the west coast of North America to resell them in China at an enormous profit, Joseph Ingraham had embarked, twice, on long transatlantic and transpacific voyages, with boats laden with sea otter furs that he intended to resell in China. During his first trip he had embarked, in 1789, an islander from Hawaii, Kalehua. He had promised to take him back to his native island on the next trip. Westerners knew that Polynesians were great navigators, capable of navigating the ocean thanks to the stars and that they knew all the islands of the Polynesian triangle, even those that Westerners did not know.

During the second voyage, which began in Boston, Joseph Ingraham had crisscrossed the Atlantic then rounded Cape Horn to enter the Pacific Ocean. He had reached the first Marquesan islands in the southeast, identified by Mendaña and visited by James Cook. Thanks to Kalehua, his Hawaiian pilot, Joseph Ingraham had continued northwest to discover, on April 19, 1791, a second group of islands, those that bear the current name of Ua Pou, Ua Huka, Nuku Hiva and Eiao.

Joseph Ingraham named the island of Nuku Hiva "Washington" and also "Franklin", because he thought he saw two islands where there was only one. Two days later, he left the archipelago, because what mattered most to him was to exchange his sea otter skins for rare and expensive products to bring back to America. Leaving the Marquesas, Joseph Ingraham headed for Hawaii where he dropped off Kalehua.

A few weeks later, a French captain, Etienne Marchand, who left Marseilles with the same idea of trading furs between North America and China, arrived at Tahuata on June 17, 1791. He continued northwest and and fell on the north-western islands, Ua Pou, Nuku Hiva, Ua Huka and Eiao. He did not know that Joseph Ingraham had just passed by and thought he was the first discoverer of these islands unknown to the Western world. He stopped at Ua Pou, while Joseph Ingraham had stopped at Nuku Hiva, the island opposite Ua Pou. He called this new archipelago "Islands of the Revolution" and took possession of it in the name of King Louis XVI. When Etienne Marchand left Marseille in 1790, Louis XVI was still the king of France. The French Revolution was only in its infancy. King Louis XVI was deposed on September 21, 1792 and beheaded on January 21, 1793.

It is a conqueror's mania. Each Western visitor who arrived on Nuku Hiva, still in its original state, appropriated the island as anyone would appropriate an object found on his way. He renamed the island in his own way, without trying to find out if the island did not already have an original name. He planted his country's flag there to make it a colony.

First, Alvaro Mendaña, in 1595, baptised the archipelago the Marquesas with this name that will remain and made it a Spanish possession. Following, in 1772, James Cook made it a possession of the British crown. In 1791, Nuku Hiva became with Joseph Ingraham an American colony under the name of Washington and with Etienne Marchand a French colony under the name of Revolution. A few years later, in

1813, with David Porter who had fallen in love with Paetini, the granddaughter of King Keitanui, Nuku Hiva was called Madison and became a possession of the United States…

In June 1835, a French megalomaniac, Charles de Thierry, who had proclaimed himself king of New Zealand under the name of Charles 1st, annexed Nuku Hiva during a visit to the Marquesas. He had his flag erected there, blue and red stamped with his coat of arms. His claims only arouse ridicule throughout the world. When Dupetit Thouars took possession of Nuku Hiva on behalf of France in 1842, Charles de Thierry unsuccessfully claimed compensation from France for having been stripped of his possessions. He will end his life in Honolulu as an employee of the French consul, in the most total oblivion.

While Western soldiers tried to subjugate Nuku Hiva with their guns and cannons, missionaries followed in their wake to impose the Christian religion. This classic duo of conquering peoples of the world is translated into a French expression by *l'alliance du sabre et du goupillon*, the alliance of the sword and the aspergillum. The goupillon or aspergillum is a small watering can used by religious to sprinkle holy water on the faithful. After the soldiers have sprinkled the natives with bullets, the religious sprinkle them with holy water.

At the end of the 17th century, the Christian religion was a baffling imbroglio. In the Pacific, two persuasions fought for religious supremacy, the Catholics and the Protestants.

The Catholic Church is one of the oldest branches of Christianity. It is governed by the Pope, world religious leader residing in Rome, Italy, with a micro-State, the Vatican, recognised by the other States of the World.

The Catholic Church has a very structured organisation on an international scale. It is the Pope and he alone who appoints the bishops, that is to say his representatives within each regional community throughout the world.

The Protestants separated from the Catholics at the beginning of the 16th century. They protested against the excesses of the Catholic Church, hence their name. Rejecting the centralised governance of the Pope, the Protestant movement is characterised by a great autonomy of the churches which compose it. This explains the variety of names by which they are known, such as Lutheran, Presbyterian, Reformed, Methodist, Evangelical, Baptist, Pentecostal...

In the conquest of the South Pacific, the Catholics initially had a head start. Alvaro Mendaña's expedition was a Catholic mission under the orders of the Pope, armed by the Catholic Kingdom of Spain.

France, which was called the eldest daughter of the Church, was also a Catholic power. However, the French Revolution in 1792 reshuffled the cards. Religious congregations were dissolved and all religious property was confiscated. The powerful organisation of the Catholic Church in France was greatly weakened.

The Catholic kingdom of Spain also saw the tide turn. The Spanish conquistadors had taken over South America 250 years earlier. The Spanish colonies bordering the Pacific served as a rear base and logistical support for the armies of the Pope, who was determined to conquer the Pacific islands. But the Spanish colonies were emancipated one after the other. Thus, Chile declared itself independent on February 12, 1818 and Peru on July 28, 1821.

The Protestants took advantage of the weak state of the Catholics to organise themselves and go on the offensive for the conquest of the pagan souls of the Pacific.

The London Missionary Society or LMS was founded in 1795, bringing together various Protestant movements, Anglicans, Methodists, Presbyterians, Baptists, Congregationalists... The LMS had set itself the ambition of converting to the Christian religion peoples of the Pacific whose existence was revealed by the navigators who crisscrossed this ocean.

The Catholic Pope having lost his French and Spanish logistical support, the English LMS had free rein to send its troops to attack the Polynesian triangle. She chartered the frigate Duff and embarked about thirty volunteers chosen to represent the ideal English society. All the trades necessary for building the mission were represented. There were masons, carpenters, but also pastors and a doctor. Some travelled with their wives and children. Le Duff left England with all these fine people on 30 September 1796, with the mission of destroying the Maohi cult and Christianising the population.

After dropping off the bulk of the troops in Tahiti on March 5, 1797, the Duff sailed to the Marquesas to disembark two last missionaries, William Pascoe Crook and John Harris. They got off at Tahuata on June 5, 1797. John Harris, frightened by the warlike aggressiveness of the inhabitants, by their cannibalistic customs and by the sexual solicitations of the Marquesan women who did not understand his refusal to sexual relations, immediately went back on board, terrified at the thought of being devoured by the cannibals after having been forced into the sin of the flesh. The sin of the flesh is the usual periphrasis of Christians to designate sexual intercourse outside of marriage.

William Crook, a 22-year-old bachelor, stood proudly when the Duff left Tahuata. He failed to convert any inhabitants. It must be said that Tahauta was infested with lawless thugs, including a Hawaiian fugitive who had teamed up with a warrior tribe to hack and loot passing whalers. These bandits did everything to frustrate the missionary's enterprise. Under the threat of being killed and eaten, William Crook fled on May 12, 1798, dressed in a simple pareo, on a small pirogue which brought him to a whaler who had just anchored. He exclaimed: "Sir, I am an Englishman and I appeal to you; if I came, it was to save my life." By saving his life, he saved the whaler from being pillaged by the pirate and his tribe who were chasing him.

The whaler dropped William Crook off at Nuku Hiva where he was better received, but where he provoked the same indifference to his religion. When he spoke of his god, the Marquesans, who love chatting a lot, spoke to him of their gods. Keitanui, one of the great chiefs of the island of Nuku Hiva, said to him: "How can you recognise a god when you don't even know how to tell the difference between two trees in the forest?" William Crook would regularly step aside to immerse himself in Bible reading. He said he was reading the word of his god. The Marquesans concluded that William Crook's representation of the god was a book, just as a tiki is a divine representation in their own culture. They concluded that William Cook was engaged in book worship.

William Crook only stayed eight months in Nuku Hiva.

William Crook's visit to the Marquesas deserves mention. He failed in his mission to convert the pagans of the Marquesas but he filled many detailed reports, intended for the LMS, in preparation for the success of a future mission. His reports provide a mine of ethnographic information on Marquesan society at a time when Western penetration had not yet led to the disappearance of more than 90% of the natives of the island and their customs.

William Crook wrote a Marquesan dictionary for use by future missionaries. He made a somewhat more accurate demographic assessment than the cursory assessments of the predecessors. He estimated that there were 90,500 inhabitants in the Marquesas Archipelago, multiplying by 3.75 the number of warriors given to him in each island. William Crook also noted that the Marquesans were in excellent health. The number of inhabitants and the health of the Marquesans will decline very quickly, in the following years, in contact with Westerners.

It was during the stay of William Crook, in 1798, that the young French sailor, Joseph Kabris, whose story is told in a previous chapter, was stranded in Nuku Hiva.

William Crook will return to Tahiti in 1816, where he founded, it is said, the city of Papeete. He was responsible for the education of Pomare III, the young king of Tahiti. The failure of William Crook in the Marquesas had been compensated by the success of the missionaries of the London Missionary Society who landed on March 5, 1797, by the Duff in Tahiti. King Pomare II was converted in 1812 and Protestantism declared the official religion of Tahiti. March 5 is a public holiday in French Polynesia, still today, in memory of the "Arrival of the Gospel". Nowadays, the followers of the religion of the missionaries of the London Missionary Society are grouped within the Maohi Protestant Church and represent 38% of the Polynesian population. This Protestant obedience, very concerned about its autonomy within the world

Protestant movement, does not hesitate to overflow the political field and to advocate the independence of French Polynesia.

William Crook's experience had convinced the LMS that it could not send European missionaries with wives and children to the Marquesas for long-term missions. Europeans could not acclimatise to such a violent society, where their lives were constantly in danger. They were very tried by the spectacle of human sacrifices and scenes of cannibalism. The idea that one of their children could be eaten was unbearable.

The LMS opted for another tactic. She decided to select from the local population individuals who showed some interest in the Christian religion, to train them in this religion and to send them on a mission to the most hostile islands. The LMS conferred them the honourable title of "teacher", which means one who teaches the word of God. Teachers were likely to be more accepted by a population whose culture they shared and to be less afraid of customs. The result of this policy has not lived up to expectations

While European culture values individual initiative, responsibility and the freedom of choice of each individual for their actions, Polynesian culture promotes collective commitment. The acceptance of a new religion could not be the affair of an individual, but of the whole community and therefore, of the will of the chief. In the minds of Polynesian chiefs, conversion to Christianity did not mean abandoning culture, beliefs, practices or ancestral rites. Conversion was a strategic means of actively associating with the domination imposed by the Western invader. The Christians' god Jehovah was just the western version of their god of war Oro.

We will find in the 20th century a spectacular reminiscence of this reflex of identity protection in the relationship that will maintain the never rusty president of French Polynesia Gaston Flosse with the tutelary power of the French State. For almost sixty years, Gaston Flosse remained at the forefront of the political scene. Although he made all kinds of political reversals, incomprehensible to a European voter, although he was prosecuted for numerous cases of illicit personal enrichment, he was always blindly followed by his voters who judged it was just a strategy to preserve the Maohi identity against overwhelming power of the French coloniser.

After the failure of William Crook, the LMS recruited and trained some Marquesans who came to Tahiti, with the aim of sending them back to convert their fellows. In 1825, William Crook accompanied them to the Marquesas Islands, to install them where he himself had preached, in the desert, one might say, thirty years earlier. A few months later, William Crook's teachers were back in Tahiti, discouraged. The reports from the LMS missionaries were clear: "The Marquesans are not ripe for conversion. These savages think only of war!"

The Marquesans were frankly resistant to certain Christian fundamentals, such as love of neighbour: "Oh no!" they said, "You must hate your enemies and kill them. If I love my enemy, he will kill me."

In the Marquesas, where the law of the strongest imposes itself on the weakest, the Christian religion, which magnifies the weakest against the strongest, aroused derision and frank disinterest. The Marquesans constantly interrupted the teachers' sermon with absurd questions: "Who is the strongest? Your god Jehovah or our own god?"

Some teachers have resumed their ancestral customs and have rebelled against the religious authority of Europeans. "Why am I going to respect the taboos of your religion, since you don't respect the taboos of my people!?" Temoana's story is particularly revealing.

On November 29, 1839, the missionaries of the LMS brought back to Nuku Hiva, his native island, a Marquesan "teacher" named Temoana whom they had disbarbarised, according to their expression, in their religious schools of Samoa and Cook.

Temoana was the grandson of the great chief Keitanui who died in 1820, this king who made fun of William Crook, this king who had welcomed Joseph Kabris, this king who had become the great king of the island thanks to guns of David Porter. Temoana was the heir to the Tei'i chiefdom of Taiohae. The Protestant pastors thought they had won the game when the Temoana's tribe built them a large dwelling in thanks for bringing their chief back. The missionaries already dreamed of making it the centre of their Nuku Hiva mission. But the case took another turn.

After five years of absence, Temoana, aged around 18, had just taken over the leadership of his tribe of Taiohae. Immediately, at the head of a thousand warriors, he attacked the neighbouring tribe of which Pakoko was the chief. Pakoko was another descendant of Keitanui and he, too, had a claim to regain the chiefdom of the whole island.

To the amazed missionaries, who believed they had transformed him into a good Christian, Temoana explained that the LMS had only been able to obtain the conversion of the people of Tahiti by converting their king Pomare, the people obeying only the king. Indeed, the LMS had baptised in the new religion the great chief

Pomare II, without having taken the trouble to rid him of barbarism then, had made him, thanks to the guns, the great king of all the other tribes of the island of Tahiti. The population had then converted to the new religion of their king. Temoana explained that for Nuku Hiva, it would be the same thing. He, Temoana, had to become the king of all the tribes and, for that, conquer them by force. Then the tribes would convert.

The attack of Temoana and his warriors was repelled by those of Pakoko. The tribe understood that the god was angry and that offerings had to be made to him. The first offerings not being enough, the warriors of Temoana captured a young man who was passing by, a Taipi who had come from the valley of Taipivai. The whole tribe gathered to perform the noisy ritual of human sacrifice. The Anglican pastor, alerted by the cries and songs of the population, ends up leaving his presbytery even though his religion forbids him any activity on the Sabbath. He discovered the population dancing around the corpse and preparing to eat it. Deeply shocked, he obtained from Temoana that the body be declared taboo so that it would not be eaten. The corpse was nevertheless dismembered and the remains exposed at the sacred places of all the tribes who had rallied to Temoana.

The warriors of Temoana did not stop there. At night, they captured two young girls from the enemy tribe. The girls were massacred with blows of head-breakers in front of the raging crowd. The corpses were exposed for two days to the violence of the members of the tribe and then hung, in full view, from the trees at the entrance to the valley.

Temoana also attacked the tribe of Hakaui on the pretext that the warriors of this tribe had kidnapped his wife. It will turn out that the wife had left her husband of her own free will. They had been married at the age of twelve and she no longer got along with him. It is in this same tribe that Pakoko took refuge in 1846 when he was pursued by French soldiers.

The instability and turmoil of the tribes that had been the experience of Nuku Hiva for centuries would persist for years to come, despite an increasingly massive infiltration of the social fabric by Westerners. The Tei'i of Taiohae were at constant war with the Taioa of Hakauì in the west, and the Hapaa and Taipi in the east.

Since the arrival of Joseph Ingraham in 1791, no European or American country and no Christian religion had succeeded in establishing a lasting authority on the island. Nuku Hiva was at the mercy of any passing profiteers.

Sandalwood had attracted international traffickers. Sandalwood is an aromatic tree that used to grow on Nuku Hiva, especially on the Toovii high plateau. The inhabitants had no particular interest in this tree. They did not know that sandalwood was, in China, a product highly sought after by practitioners of Buddhist or Taoist religions, as well as for the manufacture of traditional medicines. This unsuspected wealth had attracted traders who knew that they could resell this wood in China at a huge profit. They bought all the trees they could from the islanders until the last sandalwood disappeared in a few years. In 1990, a plan to safeguard the species was launched by the Centre for International Cooperation in Agronomic Research for Development (CIRAD) and 7.5 acres of sandalwood were replanted in Nuku Hiva.

Sperm whale fishing brought American and European whalers to the South Pacific. Nuku Hiva served as a port of call to replenish water and food supplies. The Marquesans, who were hunter-gatherers, and not farmers-breeders, often had great difficulty supplying the boats with fresh produce. The boats demanded a lot of pigs. Some unscrupulous tribal chiefs sold even the tribe's food reserves, exposing their subjects to severe food shortages.

Taking advantage of this state of lawlessness, deserters, fugitives and all sorts of adventurers have mingled with the population. They were well accepted because they brought with them technical knowledge that the natives did not master, such as the use of firearms. They brought notions of agriculture or livestock that made it possible to cope with the severe food shortages that affected the islands. They also brought alcohol and know-how ransoming and looting Western ships. The Marquesans quickly got into the habit of bartering their wealth for alcohol and guns.

The Pope, in order to counter the influence of the Protestants in Oceania, the "heretics" as he called them, organised the retaliation by creating, in 1825, a very hierarchical religious congregation, responsible for putting an end to the pagans and the heretics of Oceania. They were called the "Picpucians" because the headquarters of the organisation was on Rue Picpus in Paris. They established a rear base in Valparaiso, Chile. The first landing of the Picpucians in Nuku Hiva around 1838 ended in failure and a withdrawal to other islands. A second attempt took place in 1845, facilitated by the presence of a French military garrison and by the departure of the LMS, which threw in the towel. The success remained very limited: 104 Catholic baptisms for all the Marquesas between 1846 and 1848.

While the missionaries struggled to convince the Marquesans to adhere to the Christian faith, while the chiefs of the tribes engaged in internal wars to hit the jackpot of king of all the tribes, while the adventurers and highwaymen led the people bewildered in alcoholism and delinquency, the soldiers were preparing to submit Nuku Hiva by force to colonial law.

The French admiral Abel Dupetit-Thouars had circumnavigated the world with a stopover in the Marquesas in 1838. The King of France, Louis Philippe I, a king temporarily returned to power after the establishment of the first French Republic, had sent him to the Pacific to reconnect the great maritime dreams of the kings of France who, in competition with the kings of England, launched their warships to conquer the world.

Upon his return to France, Abel Dupetit-Thouars advised the government to annex the Marquesas in order to have a staging and supply point for warships, merchant ships and whalers. He also proposed to create a French Catholic mission to counter the influence of English Protestant missionaries. He believed that the LMS had succeeded in converting the Marquesans to Protestantism.

His proposal was accepted by the French government, which appointed Abel Dupetit-Thouars at the head of the Pacific fleet. The admiral set out again for the Marquesas archipelago. On May 1, 1842, in Tahuata, he took possession of the south-eastern Marquesas, then on June 2, 1842, in Nuku Hiva, he signed, with all the tribal chiefs, including Temoana and Pakoko, the declaration of sovereignty of France over the Northwest Marquesas. He built a garrison and a small fort, Fort Collet, on the remains of David Porter's Fort Madison, which had been destroyed three decades earlier by the popular revolt.

When Abel Dupetit-Thouars took possession of the Marquesas in 1842, he estimated its population at 15,000 inhabitants, that is to say 6 times less than the estimate made, forty years earlier, by William Crook. As for Nuku Hiva, there were only 5,000 inhabitants who had not lost their energy to fight and kill each other.

The first years of French annexation of the Marquesas were not smooth sailing. In 1844, Admiral Armand Joseph Bruat, appointed Governor of the Marquesas Islands, violently put down the revolt of the Hapaa tribe. He congratulated himself for not having any deaths on his side, but did not count the deaths on the tribe's side. This admiral will give his name to the building which today houses the presidency of French Polynesia in Tahiti.

In 1846, after the assassination of five French soldiers who had not respected a taboo in Taiohae Bay, the chief of the tribe in question, Pakoko, was shot and his warriors deported to the deserted island of Eiao. The puppet military court took the opportunity to confiscate the land of this tribe, a large part of Taiohae Bay, where the military transported their garrison and logistics. The descendants of Pakoko, including Ms. Teaki Dupont-Teikivaeoho, a businesswoman and elected representative of the Brittany region of France, where she resides, are demanding the return of the lands unjustly confiscated by France. Pakoko's royal attributes are exhibited in Paris at the Musée des Arts Premiers, Quai Branly.

In 1853, the military commander of Nuku Hiva counted only 3,150 inhabitants, including about 300 French. The military staff consisted of ten artillerymen, twelve gendarmes and a company of infantry. The French Emperor Napoleon III had sent three deportees and their families to Nuku Hiva. They were republicans who had opposed Napoleon III's coup. A penitentiary was built for the occasion, consisting of six identical houses in an easy-to-watch enclosure: three for the deportees and their families, three for the gendarmerie lieutenant and his men. The deportees were released in 1854. The penitentiary was no longer used by Napoleon III, who sent his deportees to the penal colony of Cayenne in French Guyana, opened in 1852, and to the one in New Caledonia, opened in 1864.

By 1859, the native community had been so disintegrated and shrunk by new diseases, by alcoholism and by incessant killing that it was no longer in a position to oppose organised resistance to the Westerners. The proud warriors and the beautiful Marquesan women dressed in their traditional tapa that the first discoverers of Nuku Hiva had described were nothing more than poor, dirty wretches dressed in rags who hung around the missions and garrisons.

There remained in the deep valleys less than a thousand natives who continued to live, apart, in a traditional way. They continued to fight, kill and eat each other.

The soldiers, whose number had gradually reduced over the years, left the island for good on December 15, 1859.

In gratitude for his collaboration with the French authorities, Temoana, who had opportunely been baptised in the Catholic religion in 1853, received the title of Grand Chief of Nuku Hiva, accompanied by a pension of 3,000 francs per year. After the departure of the military, the officers' mess was assigned to him as official accommodation. Temoana died of tuberculosis in 1863. His son succeeded him.

Another part of the military premises was entrusted to the religious of the Catholic mission who created a school there. It opened with about thirty pupils.

The French military authorities were seriously considering abandoning this ungovernable possession which brought nothing but trouble. But geopolitical considerations prevailed.

The French suspected the Americans of being interested in the Marquesas, which lay on an important maritime trade route between China and San Francisco. Americans, on the cover of Hawaiians, were smuggling alcohol and ammunition for guns there. They sought to maintain the indiscipline of the population and to destabilise the authority of France. This authority was only really exercised in the vicinity of Taiohae and had great difficulty in gaining respect, especially after the departure of the soldiers. Europeans dared not venture inland.

The Hawaiians had acquired vast lands and had taken up the cultivation of cotton. The Marquesan workforce being non-existent, they brought in Chinese to take care of the crops. The Chinese, victims of massacres, famines and untold misery in their country, were very eager to emigrate for a better chance of success in life. The Chinese were not slow to open stores in Taiohae and to organize the cabotage between the islands of the Marquesas.

The French knew that if they withdrew from the Marquesas, the Americans would appropriate it and create there a port and commercial platform competing with Tahiti. Indeed, the bay of Taiohae is easier to access for boats than the harbour of Papeete, in Tahiti. It is accessible even at night. On the other hand, in the second half of the 19th century, there was much talk of the drilling of the Panama Canal which would halve the journey to reach the Pacific from Europe. Nuku Hiva would then find itself on a new sea route which promised to play a very important role in international trade. It was a strategic island not to be overlooked.

Rather than leaving Nuku Hiva, the French authorities decided to organise it. In 1863, the Bishop of Tahiti and the Governor of Tahiti went together to Nuku Hiva to enact the decrees aimed at creating a civil administration. A resident-administrator and a director of indigenous affairs were appointed, placed under the high authority of the Governor of the French Establishments of Oceania. The resident-administrator represented all the administrations of the French state: expenditure authoriser civil registrar, justice of the peace, public works engineer, and even health care manager.

That year, 1863, the French navy, at the request of the bishop, repatriated dozens of Marquesans whom slave ships had captured and sold as slaves to guano miners in the coastal islands of Peru. These same slave traders had decimated the population of Easter Island, whose ancestors are Marquesans, where there were only 111 inhabitants left compared to 2,500 before their passage. Unfortunately, these freedmen brought back smallpox and died. This was the occasion to create a hospital in Taiohae. The smallpox epidemic killed about thousand deaths on Nuku Hiva despite the vaccination of the population with a vaccine sent from San Francisco. The smallpox vaccine was invented by the Englishman Edward Jenner in 1798.

In 1866, there were only a thousand inhabitants on the island.

From 1872, the civil administration of Nuku Hiva was supplemented by a civil servant who was in charge of collecting taxes and contributions. He was simultaneously treasurer-paymaster, court clerk, postmaster and notary. Title deeds to land were now subject to administrative registration as well as assignments, acquisitions and inheritances. Gradually, the administration was enriched by a port authority, a gendarmerie brigade and "mutoi", that is to say auxiliary police officers from the local population. The natives had to pay an annual tax either in kind, 10 days of work for the maintenance of roads and paths, or in money 20 francs, the salary of a day of work being worth 2 francs.

From 1870 onwards, the administrative structuring of Nuku Hiva by the French authorities, the creation of an educational and religious system by the Catholic authorities, the introduction of cash crop cotton by the Hawaiians, the creation of intra-island and inter-island trade by the Chinese facilitated the adoption of new social norms by the natives. The Marquesans dressed and adopted the clothes in vogue in Tahiti. Some began to cultivate their own land. They had rediscovered the smile, the cheerfulness and the sympathetic eagerness towards foreigners that had made the legend of their forefathers a century earlier. Leaving the tribal model, the Marquesans adopted the parochial model, that is to say a village centred by a church and a school.

Only 1% of the population had survived the arrival of the Westerners a century earlier. It will be necessary to wait until the year 1930 and the improvement of health services, to observe a repopulation of Nuku Hiva by its highly mixed original population. The number of inhabitants, in 2022, has not yet exceeded 3,000.

5 - HEIKE'S STORYTELLING

Heike recounted what happened in various press interviews as well as in a book where she recounts her life with Stefan and her journey around the world.

When Heike and Stefan anchored their catamaran in Hakatea Bay on Saturday 8, October 2011, there were no other boaters. They were amazed by the grandiose spectacle of the bay, surrounded by high mountains, barred by a sandy beach, bordered with a row of coconut trees.

Arriving in the bay, Heike and Stefan already had an idea of what they were going to find and had set themselves some goals for this stage.

With their dinghy, Heike and Stefan went ashore. They walked on the beach aimlessly. They found a path on which they embarked. Here and there were lemon trees scenting the air. They picked these little lime, green and yellow lemons, which the Marquesans use to enhance their raw fish dish, but which boaters put in the Caribbean ti 'punch, as an aperitif with friends. Continuing along the trail, Heike and Stefan arrived at the hamlet of Hakaui. There was no living soul, just a few makeshift dwellings, the rusty sheet metal roofs, the plywood walls, sometimes painted a pastel blue or green, the windows open to the wind.

A little further down the path, they passed a young man, very simply dressed, shirtless, with his horse. He was a Marquesan, as described in the books, tall, tanned, muscular, with black hair and eyes. He had a large traditional tattoo on his left shoulder and on his left arm. In the imagination of Heike and Stefan, the Marquesans were happy, sociable, welcoming beings, living in a heavenly world. There was no doubt that this young man was the Marquesan to meet. They decided to contact him. His name was Arihano.

The next day, Stefan and Heike set off on a hike in the Hakaui Valley to visit the Vaipo waterfall, a two-hour walk from the beach. Vaipo is one of the places that all boaters who stop in Hakatea Bay must go. The spectacle is striking. At the bottom of the valley, the waterfall falls from a ledge of the mountain into a basin, over a height of one thousand three hundred feet. The basin feeds the small stream that flows peacefully down to the beach in the bay.

Back from their hike, around noon, Heike and Stefan met Arihano again in the hamlet of Hakaui. Stefan had in mind to hunt the wild goat. It was a project on his wish list to implement in the Marquesas. Stefan could already see himself telling this epic hunt, to his amazed colleagues and friends, when he returned to Germany. He had tried his luck twice in Fatu Hiva, but it hadn't worked. He asked Arihano to take him goat hunting. He himself had a shotgun and offered Arihano to take it. Arihano had his and that was enough.

Two hours later, Arihano was ready. He had returned to the beach and whistled in the direction of the catamaran to call Stefan. Heike saw them disappear into the coconut grove, each carrying their backpack with everything they needed to hunt and bivouac.

As night fell, Heike heard someone calling her. It was Arihano approaching the catamaran, aboard the dinghy that had remained on the beach. Arihano knew a few words of English and Heike a few words of French. Communication was laborious. She asked "Where is Stefan?" and she understood Arihano's words "accident... forest..." She jumped into the dinghy, very worried about Stefan's fate, and ran into the forest after Arihano.

After a quarter of an hour, the path had vanished. She exclaimed, very worried, "Where's Stefan?" Arihano made a gesture that meant "I don't know". Heike got angry and swore at Arihano in English and German, but the only word Arihano could understand was "idiot". Heike, planting Arihano there, turned around on the path and began to call Stefan with all his might. But no response.

The night was dark and she couldn't see the path. She stopped, heart pounding, listening to Stefan's slightest call. The crackle of dry leaves and twigs warns her of Arihano's approach. Arihano pops up pointing the gun at his head. She immediately understood the violent words that came out of his mouth "I'm going to kill you".

"No!" she cried, snatching the gun from him. He jumped on her and she struggled violently. Arihano was bigger and stronger. He threw her to the ground, face down, sat on her back, grabbed her head by the hair and, in a fit of rage, began banging her head hard against the ground. Then he grabbed her neck with both hands and strangled Heike until she had no more strength to resist. He released the hold. Inert and half-conscious, Heike felt Arihano's hands go under her T-shirt and in her panties, kneading her breasts and searching her sex. Then he lay on top of her, rubbing his cock violently against her body until he ejaculated.

Arihano's violence then subsided. He straightened Heike and motioned for her to breathe calmly, to come to her senses. He gave her water to drink. She tried to argue with him, but he did not understand and, anyway, was not interested in what she was saying, moved by his diabolical plan.

Arihano dragged Heike to the foot of a tree, his back against the trunk. He tied his hands to the back of the trunk with the cord provided to bring the goat back. With another rope, he went around the trunk and neck, tightly pinning Heike to the tree. He gagged her with a T-shirt that tasted badly burnt. She thought Arihano was going to cut her to pieces with his menacing machete, but he disappeared into the forest.

The moon had risen in the sky and the night was no longer so dark. Heike tried to break free by wriggling in all directions. Arihano returned soon after. His face grimacing with rage, he began to scream violently against Heike's face, mimicking the gesture of slicing his neck with his machete. Heike was paralysed. After checking the links, Arihano went back to the forest.

When she no longer heard Arihano's footsteps, after she had the feeling that he had gone away, Heike more methodically resumed his work of liberation. Gradually she managed to slip her right hand out of the bonds and then to undo the other knots. She took a few steps. The twigs and dry leaves crackled so loudly under her every step that she dared not move forward for fear that Arihano would hear her. She was wondering where to hide when she saw in the distance, between the trees, the swing of the light beam from Arihano's torch. He was approaching.

Panicking, she began to run headlong in the opposite direction. She bumped into the branches; she tripped over the roots. She got up immediately. She lost one shoe and then the other, not trying to get them back. She had only one idea, to run, to run as far as possible. Thorns, angular stones pierced her feet, but panicked at the idea that Arihano could catch her, she no longer felt any pain.

Exhausted, she stopped to catch her breath. She didn't know where she was. But suddenly, the scent of lemon trees crossed the forest. She was no longer far from the beach.

Guided by the backwash of the waves, she ran to the beach and plunged into the waves without looking back, fearing to see the beam of Arihano's torch appear among the coconut trees.

Despite her exhaustion, she swam vigorously away from the beach, driven by a violent survival instinct that erased her pain and fatigue. She did not dare to return to her catamaran, fearing that Arihano would come to find her there. Far away in the bay, there was a second yachtsman who had arrived during the day. It was far. Ten times she thought she was dying, drowned with fatigue or devoured by sharks attracted by the blood from her wounds.

This boat belonged to a Dutchman who knew Heike and Stefan and had become friends with the German couple as they met in their transoceanic wanderings. The Dutchman sensed that something was wrong. When he arrived in the bay, he saw that Heike and Stefan's catamaran was unoccupied, with the accesses not closed, unlike what boaters do when they leave the boat for an excursion or an invitation. He did not see them on the beach. At nightfall, his presentiment turned into worry, because nothing had moved on his friends' catamaran, whose lights remained off.

When he noticed, under the brightness of the moon, someone struggling in the water, he exclaimed "Heike!?". Heike heard his name called. She felt enormous relief. The hellish chase was over and she wasn't going to die...

After getting Heike to safety on the boat, the Dutch friend called the gendarmes with his satellite phone.

The gendarmes are based in the village of Taiohae. They arrived with their speedboat two hours later, because there is no other access than the sea to reach Hakatea Bay from Taiohae. They went in search of Stefan and Arihano, but in the night they found nothing. On Monday, they resumed the search and they found nothing. On Tuesday, same failure. But on Tuesday, a reinforcement from the gendarmerie arrived from Tahiti with a tracking dog.

On Wednesday, the gendarmes asked Heike to come to Taiohae to be informed of the follow-up to the investigation. They had discovered in an isolated area the ashes of a large brazier, larger than the one hunters make to cook slaughtered goats. In the midst of the extinguished embers and ashes, there were remains, incompletely charred, of animal or human flesh. But there were also half-melted metal objects, a dental prosthesis, buttons of clothing, belt buckles. Heike recognized all these objects and there was no doubt that they were indeed Stefan's remains. However, the gendarmes asked her to wait for the forensic investigation to have confirmation.

6 - ARIHANO'S ESCAPE

Arihano will disappear for fifty days before surrendering to the gendarmes. He had an excellent knowledge of the island of Nuku Hiva where he was born. He knew well the methods of survival in difficult environment. He was accustomed to bivouac, several days in a row, in pursuit of wild goats, in the most remote places of the mountain.

The island of Nuku Hiva is not very big. Eighteen miles long by nine wide, it is the size of the island of Malta in the Mediterranean or Grenada in the Caribbean and twice that of Honolulu in the Pacific. Despite Arihano's ability to survive, hidden, in a mountainous region, it was obvious that he had been able to escape the gendarmes on his heels because he benefited, in a discreet way, from the solidarity of his people.

Arihano had a good reputation. He belonged to a well-known and respected family from Nuku Hiva. His father, a municipal truck driver, was a respected pillar of the island's Catholic community. One of his cousins, who bears the same surname as him, had become the she companion of the President of French Polynesia, Gaston Flosse, that never rusty politician who, since the 1960s, has never ceased to be at the forefront of the media, both political and judicial. Gaston Flosse, with his population, had the aura of a great tribal chief just like the great chief Keitanui who, 230 years earlier, had faced the invasion of Nuku Hiva by Westerners.

Arihano had returned to live with his father in Nuku Hiva, three months before the events, following the breakup of his nurse friend in Tahiti. She had let him down. He, without a job, had no income to live on. Arihano was a reputedly nice guy and no one wanted to believe that he could have committed a horrible crime.

Arihano had a criminal record. He was sentenced in 2005 to six months in prison for a burglary. There is something folkloric about being imprisoned in Nuku Hiva. The island prison is the smallest prison in France. It is a building, resembling a dwelling house, without surrounding wall or watchtower. It has five cells. It has a director and three guards in all. The guards are Marquesans themselves.

Originally, the prison building was the general store that the French navy had built, immediately after the signing, on June 1, 1842, between Admiral Abel Dupetit-Thouars and Grand Chief Temoana, grandson of King Keitanui, accompanied by the chiefs of the vassal tribes, of the "Declaration of the Chiefs of Nukahiva Island for the Recognition of French Sovereignty". This building, after the departure of the French soldiers, had served for some time as official accommodation for the great chief Temoana to whom the French paid a pension.

The atmosphere inside the prison of Nuku Hiva is almost family. During the day, the cell doors are open and the detainees can walk freely inside and outside in the garden, under the relaxed supervision of the guard on duty. The detainees do their cooking, clean the premises and maintain the garden. They receive family and friends under a mango tree. In the evening, the prisoners go back to their cell and the guard goes home. Life in Taiohae prison resembles that of a high school student who would stay in boarding school during the holidays without the possibility of returning to his parents.

There are never any problems in Taiohae prison. A prisoner who does not play the game would be sent back to Nuutania prison, in Tahiti. The Nuutania prison, unlike that of Nuku Hiva, was classified, in the 2010s, by the International Observatory of Prisons, as the most dilapidated and the most overcrowded of the prisons in France. The conditions of detention there were considered the most inhumane and degrading in the French rankings.

The function of the singular prison of Nuku Hiva is to show the inhabitants that, when one of their own commits an offence, justice punishes him in full view of all. It is the punishment of the bad pupil, like that of the schoolmaster who put an unruly pupil in the corner of the class. Once the punishment has been carried out, the pupil returns to his place and all is forgotten. The population no longer held it against Arihano for the fault that had sent him to prison six years earlier.

This fateful Sunday, October 9, 2011, while the gendarmes searched the valley of Hakaui, in search of him and that of Stefan, Arihano, who knew the passages used by the wild goats, escaped by climbing the cliff to find himself on the Toovii plateau, two thousand five hundred feet above sea level.

The Toovii plateau corresponds to the half-collapsed bottom of the crater of the volcano, which has been extinct for two million years. It is from this plateau that flows the Vaipo waterfall in the Haikaui valley. The climate of the plateau is much cooler than that of the coastal villages. The hilly landscape is covered with meadows and forests. It is not inhabited. The Marquesans leave their cattle there for grazing.

On the plateau, Arihano found, in a refuge, a young shepherd who took care of the horses and cows of his family. The young Marquesan later explained to the gendarmerie that he had neither radio nor television and that he was not aware that Arihano was wanted. He found it normal for Arihano to make a stopover in this refuge to stock up on food and clothing, as do hunters who are preparing to bivouac for several days in the mountains. The young man had only learned when he returned to the village that Arihano was wanted.

When the young shepherd returned, Arihano's friends had gone to find him in his hiding place on the Toovii plateau. Arihano was no longer there. The friends found a scribbled message: "I did something wrong. It's not okay. You must help me."

The inhabitants of Nuku Hiva were under a double shock, the shock of the murder and the rape of which Arihano was accused, the shock of the press articles which treated the Marquesans as a primitive and cannibal tribe. Humiliated by the racist remarks of the Western press and, moreover, of the French press which had taken part in the launch of the quarry, the Marquesans immediately felt the need to protect one of their own from the hunt undertaken by the gendarmerie.

The gendarmerie is a military institution responsible for maintaining order and respect for the law throughout the French national territory. In the eyes of Polynesians, the gendarme is the embodiment of the French state. He is the armed wing of France to colonise Polynesia and impose its law.

The Marquesans are respectful of the law and have no desire for independence, unlike their cousins in Tahiti. They are satisfied with the management of their island by the French state. It was not the exacerbation of an independence movement that led the Marquesans not to deliver Arihano to the judicial authority. Treated as cannibals and primitives by the entire Western press, they had the strong feeling that Arihano, like them, was the victim of an international vendetta.

When the gendarmes asked them if they had noticed anything, people said that they had more or less recognised Arihano in such and such a place. It was always a while later and Arihano had disappeared when the gendarmes went to check the information.

The Marquesans had made Arihano their Robin Hood, who, each time the gendarmes were about to catch him, managed to disappear. It was said that at night, in order to change his hiding place, he crawled on paths traced by the ancestors. It was said to feed on guavas, very abundant on the island, and wild plants like the ancients. It was said that he captured wild goats for food, making traps with rudimentary means. It was said that the moment the tracker dog tracked him down, he disappeared under the water, breathing on a reed stalk.

In front of the press, the Marquesans were offended at not being invited by the authorities to participate in the search, because they knew, better than the gendarmes, they said, the possible hiding places. But the gendarmes quickly realised that Arihano was slipping through their fingers because he was benefiting from the help of the inhabitants. The gendarmerie broadcast messages on the radio threatening legal action against those who helped the fugitive.

Arihano had left the Toovii plateau to hide in Terre Déserte" [Desert Land], in a deep gorge that opens onto the ocean. The small torrent in the valley provided him with fresh water. As its name suggests, this part of the island is desert due to the harshness of its relief. There is no permanent habitat, with the exception of the island's airport, which was built on one of the few flat areas accessible without danger to planes. The airport is quite far from the valley where Arihano had taken refuge and is separated from it by a steep relief. No road leads to this valley. Those who helped Arihano and those who sought him could only arrive by sea. Arihano watched from afar. He would show up if a friend arrived. He fled if the maritime launch of the gendarmerie appeared.

Arihano's escape is reminiscent of that of his ancestor Pakoko. The history of Pakoko is well preserved in the memory of the Marquesans of Nuku Hiva. The descendants of this chief parade, nowadays, under his name to denounce the spoliation of the lands of his tribe pronounced by the court which had condemned him to death. Arihano's family home is on the tribal lands of Pakoko.

Pakoko was the chief of the Hikoei, Haavao and Pakiu tribes on Taiohae Bay. On January 28; 1845, French military sailors, who had just arrived on the island and did not know the taboo, had gone to the mouth of the Pakiu Valley River to bathe and wash their clothes. The Pakoko warriors surrounded them and killed five of them.

The version transmitted by oral tradition is more epic. French soldiers had grabbed Pakoko's daughter and raped her. Pakoko, angry, had killed six of them with his head breaker.

The naked bodies of the soldiers, fixed on a pole in the manner of human sacrificial victims, had been transported to the places of worship and the head of one of them, exposed for all to see. The military commander, in retaliation, attacked and burned the village of Pakoko. Pakoko had taken refuge, with his warriors, among the Hapaa, in the valley of Hakaui, this valley where Stefan disappeared. To go from the valley of Taiohae to the valley of Hakaui, Pakoko had crossed the high mountain ridge which separates them. The military commander had sent about 60 soldiers to capture the fugitives. Fearing that their village would be destroyed, the high priestess of the Haapa predicted a great famine if Pakoko and his warriors did not surrender. The French soldiers, informed of the surrender of the fugitives, had withdrawn. A few days later, Pakoko returned to Taiohae and surrendered with five of his warriors. Pakoko had been found guilty of murder and sentenced to death by the military tribunal. Recognizing the crime, he had accepted the punishment reserved for warriors. He didn't want to be hanged, but shot. Refusing to have his eyes blindfolded and his hands tied, he had waited for the mortal salvo with a certain detachment, his chef's fan in his hand. This happened on March 21, 1845. His Grand Chief attributes are now on display in Paris at the Musée des Arts Premiers.

Arihano, located by his pursuers, left the ravine of Terre Déserte for a place more accessible to his supporters. He had hidden in the vicinity of the Vaikave waterfall. This waterfall is a tourist site of Terre Déserte, isolated and little frequented, accessible on foot from the road crossing the island. This road connects Taiohae Bay to the airport. It is a very winding track that winds through the middle of mountain ranges and runs along impressive precipices. Its coating is irregular, often damaged by bad weather or landslides. Vehicles drive with caution.

From the heights of the Vaikave waterfall, Arihano could see, in the distance, the vehicles slowly descending from the high ridge separating the Toovii plateau from Terre Déserte.

The gendarmes had ended up locating Arihano in Vaikave thanks to telephone tapping of those who were likely to help him. They tried to catch it by leading an expedition at dawn. But Arihano detected their approach and managed to flee into the mountains by taking goat paths.

Arihano's last hiding place was located on the mountain above Taiohae Bay, not far from the Tekeika panoramic site. This belvedere, two thousand feet above sea level, is also called "Point de vue Melville", named after the famous American writer Herman Melville, who wrote a novel about the Taipi tribe, one of the great tribes of Nuku Hiva. It is a must-see stop for all tourists arriving from the airport by taxi. This lookout offers a breath-taking view of Taiohae Bay.

From this hiding place, Arihano had a view of the gendarmerie and witnessed all the preparations of the gendarmes who were looking for him. He then had time to disappear into the most inaccessible heights of the mountain.

His friends discreetly brought him food. It is in this hiding place that Arihano made the decision to end his run.

On November 28, 2011, the fifty-first day of his disappearance, Arihano showed up at his father's house. "I can't take it anymore," he told him.

The very religious father was imbued with the parable of the prodigal son, attributed to Jesus Christ and told by his disciples in the Gospels.

Jesus said: A man had two sons. The youngest said to his father: my father, give me my share of the inheritance. The father shared his property with them. The young son, having collected everything, went to a remote region, where he dissipated his inheritance by living in debauchery. When he had spent it all, a great famine arose. The young son found himself in need and no one wanted to feed him. He said to himself: everyone at my father's has plenty of bread, and I, here, am starving! I will return to my father and I will say to him – My father, I have sinned against heaven and against you, and I am no longer worthy to be called your son; treat me as one of your slaves. - He got up and went to his father. While he was still far away, his father saw him and was moved with compassion, he ran to throw himself on his neck and kissed him. The son said to him – My father, I have sinned against heaven and against you, I am no longer worthy to be called your son. - But the father, instead of reprimanding him, said to the whole family - Let us rejoice. My son was like dead and he came back alive! He was lost, and he is found!

Arihano and his father knelt down and prayed. Then the father called the gendarmes.

The public prosecutor in Tahiti immediately announced to the media that the Nuku Hiva gendarmerie had received a call from his father at around 7 p.m., telling them that his son was at home and that he wanted to surrender.

7 - ARIHANO'S STORYTELLING

To the gendarmes, Arihano gave the account of what happened before he fired a shotgun at Stefan and killed him. His account sounded so absurd that the court, made up of Western judges, did not believe a word of it.

Arihano and Stefan come from different cultures that have different use of storytelling.

In Western culture, the storytelling, to be believable, must be logical. The one who comes out of a rational approach passes for a liar or a poet or a storyteller or a mentally deranged or a man of the Church. The best support for the storytelling is the written word, because it stabilises its content, as the saying goes: "The words fly away, the writings remain". When a gendarme hears a witness or an accused, he systematically writes a report of the hearing. Everything that may have been said orally during the hearing and which was not reported in the minutes vanishes. In the procedure, only the written document prevails.

Polynesian culture developed without writing until the arrival of Europeans. Polynesians have always shared their ideas, their feelings or their knowledge by using the word accompanied by feelings and emotions, such as joy, anger, fear, sadness, disgust, surprise. Words alone are not enough to make a storytelling believable. This is why, in Polynesian culture, writing does not have the same success as in Western culture. Rather than reading a user manual, the Polynesian prefers to hear the explanation given by someone who knows. The primacy of feeling, for understanding the information circulating within the community, appears in the answers of Polynesians questioned about the activity of their elected representatives. Many of them say: "We don't know anything. They didn't come to tell us?", while the explanations are detailed in the newspapers or in information leaflets or on billboards.

In the Polynesian world, belief in the storytelling is a felt experience, made up of words that touch the reason and feelings that touch the heart. The very old French philosopher, Blaise Pascal, translated the duality of belief by his famous aphorism "The heart has its reasons that reason ignores". Blaise Pascal meant that in order to believe in the religious narrative, one had to abandon reason and rely on one's heart. It is Westerners who think that the heart is the place where feelings are born and die.

Rational reasoning and the written word are the western means of communication. The Polynesian is deeply annoyed by the coldness of these means. To communicate, he prefers words and feelings. He does not hesitate to make forays into the imagination to dress his story with feelings and emotions, in order to make it conducive to the acceptance of the listener. The Polynesian narrative is inherently unstable, as it can vary from one interlocutor to another.

The dissection of Arihano's narrative, after discarding the additions of his imagination, allows the reconstruction of the scenario of the real facts. Stefan didn't speak French and Arihano didn't speak English or German. Each had a rough understanding of what the other was saying to him. Each interpreted the words and gestures of the other according to their own cultural experience.

Initially, Arihano had no intention of homicide. He had no intention of robbing Stefan. Just like Stefan, he wanted to have a good time and he was very happy to be able to show a foreigner his country and his culture. The trip began under good omens.

When Arihano and Stefan arrived at the basin at the foot of the Vaipo waterfall, they stopped. They bathed in the basin, Stefan naked, as is the custom of the Germans.

For Arihano, being completely naked is much more difficult, because, in his community, there is a religious prohibition that is translated into everyday language by the expression "It's shameful". At the time of the colonisation of the Pacific islands, Europeans considered that the nudity of the islanders was an obvious criterion of an uncivilised people. Walking around with one's sex visible was a primitive behaviour, close to that of animals, since animals do not hide anything about their sex, their sexuality and their urinary and faecal excreta. In the late 1790s, British Protestant missionaries from the London Missionary Society, the first Christian missionaries to land on Nuku Hiva, undertook to change this way of being which they considered indecent and immoral. The Marquesans, vexed at being reduced to the rank of animals, got into the habit of wearing clothes that hid their sex.

For Stefan, bathing naked with Arihano was a return to the candour of the original peoples, so praised by the accounts of the first Western sailors who visited the

Pacific.

For Arihano, bathing naked with Stefan was a return to the primitive state that the colonizer had made him feel ashamed of.

After the swim, Arihano made a fire. He and Stefan sat down and drank alcohol. They talked, each in his own linguistic and gestural gibberish.

Stefan, who had arrived in the Marquesas six weeks earlier, had watched the preparations for a festival of traditional songs and dances for a long time. The male and female dancers are dressed in vegetal outfits which reveal, with each movement, their naked body, with the exception of the sex which is carefully hidden. They perform, to the sound of the toere, the traditional drums, combat scenes and very suggestive sexual parades. Westerners strongly feel the erotic character of the show. The missionaries of the London Missionary Society considered the dances practiced by the tribes satanic and obscene. As early as 1815, they drew on the Bible to enact written codes that prohibited the most satanic customs, including tribal dancing. The Catholic Christian religious fathers who succeeded, in 1845, the Protestant missionaries who had thrown in the towel trying to Christianize this unruly people, maintained the ban on tribal cultural events. The French Catholics were more successful than the British Protestants, the presence of a French military garrison facilitating the respect of the laws of the coloniser which were confused with the laws of religion. It was not until the 1980s that Marquesans dared to reclaim the dances of their ancestors.

Stefan, like all visitors to the Marquesas, was moved by the body of the dancers. He was steeped in the tales of early Western sailors who described islanders happy, welcoming and living a completely liberated and unbridled sexuality. In these stories, the Marquesan women of yesteryear offered their bodies to passing sailors, without restraint and without compensation, without the men of the island taking offence.

All of this was spinning in Stefan's head when he saw Arihano, half-naked, athletic and tattooed, walking in front of him on the path to the valley, swimming with him in the Vaipo basin and making a fire for him to take a rest.

In conversation they talked about sex. Stefan made Arihano the proposal to implement a fantasy that had matured in his head.

In the top 10 of male homosexual fantasies, we find that of domination-submission. Excitement is greatest when the stronger and more dangerous is bound by bonds and subjected to the domination of the weaker. Arihano was tall and athletic and Stefan was frailer. It was Arihano who let himself be tied up and it was Stefan who sodomised him. In ancient tales, it was the cannibal of Nuku Hiva who caught the stranded sailor and ate him. What a beautiful fantasy, for Stefan, to imagine the stranded sailor who captures a cannibal and sodomises him.

In Germany, homosexuality is socially accepted. A German man, even if he is heterosexual, assumes without difficulty an occasional homosexual relationship. Stefan had already had homosexual experiences in Germany. His partner, Heike, knew this and it was not an obstacle to their life as a couple.

For Arihano, assuming a homosexual relationship is difficult. The Protestant and Catholic religious who Christianised the Marquesas completely washed away the original Marquesan culture. The ban on homosexuality has struck all Judeo-Christian religions for millennia. "A man should not have sex with a man as a man has with a woman. It's horrible," reads the biblical texts that were written 2,500 years ago and are considered God's teaching to his people. These texts brought together under the name of Bible for Christians and Torah for Jews serve as a reference for social and religious life for believers. Sodomy is therefore part of the satanic customs that the missionaries of the London Missionary Society immediately wanted to eradicate. The word "sodomy" has long been used to designate male homosexual relations, female homosexual relations having interested neither religions nor legislators. In the kingdom of France, until the French Revolution in 1791, the crime of sodomy was punished by burning at the stake. It was not until 1982 that the French parliament clearly decriminalised homosexuality. In 1990, the World Health Organisation removed homosexuality from the list of mental illnesses.

he Marquesans, from the 1980s, began to defy religious prohibitions, to reclaim the customs of their ancestors, such as singing, dancing and tattoos. But homosexuality remained in the forbidden zone, described as unnatural behaviour.

Arihano could not publicly admit that he had had a consensual same-sex relationship with Stefan. He risked the reprobation and discredit of his community. So he said that this relationship was forced on him by Stefan, at gunpoint.

A journalist during the trial asked his lawyer: "Are you going to try to show that the accused was sexually assaulted and that, in revenge, he killed Stefan? The lawyer replied, "This is what Arihano has been arguing from the start. This is his first version; he repeated it several times. There is a point on which he differed on this rape, but which can be explained quite simply: would it make you happy for others to know that you were sodomised by another man? Nope! He felt that he was ashamed of it and that may explain this isolated version change, because, throughout the investigation, he will confirm that it went well."

Although Westerners have always had strong reluctance to talk about it in their stories, homosexual relationships existed in the Polynesian world long before the arrival of Westerners in the Pacific. Here is what one could read in the account of a traveller dating from 1804: "There is a class of individuals whose profession is so abominable that the delicacy of our language and decency do not allow us to make it known. The natives give these men the name of Mahoos. They dress like women, affect their manners, caprices and coquetry. They usually live in their society and are much sought after. With women's costumes and mannerisms, they adopted their labours. They sew, spin and, in a word, they look so much like them for their effeminate look that if they hadn't been introduced to me, I would have taken them for women." This traveller, refusing, in the name of decency, to describe their sexual mores in French, continues in Latin, *Injicunt penem in orem...*, to explain that they put men's penises in their mouths and swallow the sperm.

The Mahus survived Christianization. In all families, there is always a boy who takes on effeminate attitudes early on and orients himself towards typically feminine activities and games. In adulthood, the Mahus enjoy the professions of home help, education, fashion, choreography, crafts.

More recently, as an extension of the Mahu culture, the phenomenon of Raerae has developed. Raeraes are male transgenders who live in female gender. While the

Mahu perfectly assumes his male sex, he chooses to live in a relationship with a woman and have children, the Raerae considers himself a woman living, by mistake, in the skin of a man. The Raerae is more maximalist than the Mahu. He uses feminising hormones to increase the volume of his breasts and decrease his male sexual characteristics. He does not hesitate to have breast prostheses fitted and, if he has the means, to resort to castration surgery and the creation of a vagina. He is looking for life in a relationship with a rather virile man.

In ancient times, the Mahu had the role of sex education for young people. Teenagers had complete sexual freedom and the occurrence of a teenage pregnancy was always welcome. Nowadays, Raeraes offers their services, without much exclusivity, to men who need to satisfy a desire for sexual intercourse. It is a resurgence of the ancestral custom. In communities far from urban centres, this service to the population is not remunerated. The Raerae plays a pacifying role, because by bringing a male, stuffed with testosterone, to orgasm, it causes his aggressiveness to drop.

Like all his congeners, Arihano had already had sexual relations with Raeraes from Nuku Hiva. The latter admitted it without difficulty, but Arihano did not recognise it.

Stefan knew that alcohol would disinhibit Arihano and help him break through the taboo of same-sex relationships. During his interrogation by the investigators, Arihano rather than acknowledging his active participation in the sexual game proposed by Stefan, said that he had put up no resistance because the alcohol had put him in a daze.

Arihano's description of his rape by Stefan appeared far-fetched and no one believed him. Arihano explained that Stefan threatened him with the gun and tied him to the tree with one leg in the air.

This position, where one leg is held in the air by a rope while the other rests on the ground, supporting the whole weight of the body in a somewhat unstable way, is a classic in BDSM clubs, that is to say, Bondage, Discipline, Submission, Sado-Masochism. These clubs, which exist across Europe, allow its followers to act out fantasies that use pain, coercion and humiliation to induce sexual arousal. BDSM practice is based on a codified contract between the players. In role-playing, there are those who play the role of master, dominant, sadist and those who play the role of submissive, slave, masochist. The club's environment makes it possible to define a contract that does not put the lives of others in danger, to secure its progress in order to avoid serious injury, and to interrupt it in the event of non-compliance with the clauses.

Arihano could not recognise, in front of the investigators and in front of his community, his consent to play the role of the submissive captive. He has therefore fashioned a hard version where submission is imposed on him. He said: "Stefan held the rifle in one hand while he tied me up with the other". The scene could never be reproduced during the reconstruction of the murder before the investigating judge. It was impossible to hold the rifle in one hand and fasten intricate links with the other.

Arihano, unable to say that he had voluntarily participated in this BDSM simulacrum to the end, will explain to the gendarmes that he had lost consciousness when Stefan sodomised him.

The investigating judge, like the court, never believed such nonsense. It is this version that Arihano circulated on the island to his friends who came to his aid. This version was immediately adopted by the inhabitants of the island, because it reinforced the cliché, very fashionable, of the foreigner who goes to Polynesia with the aim of sexual predation.

Arihano will continue to develop with the gendarmes this presentation which made him the victim of a Western sexual predator. He will explain that he had managed to break free from his bonds, that he had picked up the gun that Stefan had left on the ground and that he had shot Stefan for fear of being raped again. Stefan had collapsed in the fire and his body had burned.

In reality, it is more likely that Stefan and Arihano continued to drink after this sexe game and that Arihano had an uncontrolled reaction, triggered by an inappropriate statement or attitude from Stefan.

This kind of violent and uncontrolled reaction, which causes the death of a man, is well known in the legal circles of Polynesia. In September 2006, Tahiti had been shaken by a murder which has some analogies with that of Stefan. Dr Patrice S., a French nephrologist in his forties, had been practising in Tahiti for fifteen years. He was an affable man, appreciated by his patients for his kindness and availability. He lived without ostentation in the suburbs of Papeete. His naked body was found on Monday, September 4, 2006, lying in a pool of blood. The murder appeared very violent, for the body bore the marks of an enraged fury. The murderer was quickly confused, as he had used the doctor's credit card to make purchases and his presence had been repeatedly noticed by the neighbourhood. He was a 29-year-old Polynesian who, like Arihano, had a low level of education. He did not have a regular job, but lived with his wife and two children in a disadvantaged neighbourhood in another township. For six months, the doctor and he had, unbeknownst to everyone, a weekly sexual relationship, every Friday. The murder had taken place on the Friday before the body was found. When investigators asked the Polynesian to explain why he had killed the doctor with whom he got along so well and with whom he regularly shared a good sexual time, he gave a surprising explanation. As the two of them sat calmly side by side, drinking a beer, the doctor joked while patting him on the head in a friendly way. The Polynesian had then felt rising in him a destructive and uncontrollable rage. He had, blindly and without restraint, beaten his lover with violent punches and kicks until his strength and his rage were exhausted. The doctor was dead a few hours later. He lived alone, no one had been able to save him.

Can a friendly slap on the back of the head trigger deadly violence? Yes, if we refer to ancient Polynesian customs which attributed to the head a role very different from the Western conception. Ancient Polynesian statuary, the tiki, represents human forms with a huge head, disproportionate to the rest of the body.

In Polynesian cosmogony, the head is not the place of thought and feelings, a role attributed to the belly, but the place of passage of "mana". Mana is a concept specific to Polynesian culture. It is the vital principle which gives the capacity to live to all beings and to all things. To eat one's neighbour is to acquire one's mana, that is to say, all his power and vital force. Polynesian cosmogony has some similarities with Christian cosmogony. There is a supreme god and sub-divinities who are usually located in the darkness of the starry sky. Each star corresponds to a human being. A shooting star indicates a change in the status of this human being, his death, for example. The same kind of association between human beings and stars can be found in the Western expression "to be born under a lucky star" to mean "to be lucky". The Polynesian ancestral religion, like the Christian religion, believed in a form of supernatural survival beyond death. The head was the place where everyone's mana connected with the mana of all beings in the supernatural world.

We find an identical cosmogony in the Christian myth of Easter and Pentecost. Jesus had been crucified by the Romans a few days before the Jewish holiday of Easter. On Easter Day, his body had disappeared from the tomb. His disciples explained that Jesus had risen and ascended to heaven to join the supreme god, called God the Father. Jesus was God the Son and he had gone to join his father. On the day of the Jewish feast of Pentecost, fifty days after that of Easter, many faithful, coming from different regions, had gathered, in Jerusalem, in the house where Jesus had taken, before dying, a last meal with his first twelve disciples. Suddenly, a violent clap of thunder had filled the whole house where they were sitting. The lightning caused optical phenomena, known to scientists as orbs, to form in the room. The disciples interpreted this phenomenon as tongues of fire that rested on the head of each disciple. They considered that God the Father transmitted, in this way, to each disciple, knowledge of divine origin, unknown to other human beings. The disciples called this communication between the supernatural and the natural the Holy Spirit. This is why the disciples of Jesus are represented with a flame above their heads.

In traditional Polynesian social relations, the top of the head was taboo. It was forbidden, with an undue gesture, to break the connection of the individual mana with the network of the supernatural mana. On pain of death, only the mother, or the traditional priest, the taua, could touch the head of her child. If a child stood across the entrance to a hut, do not step over it, but pick it up, enter it and put it back where it was. Do not stretch an object over the head of an individual, but pass next to him.

An assumed homosexual Polynesian, who listened to the story of the doctor's murder, triggered by a friendly pat on the head, reacted very emotionally, because he had experienced the same situation. While he was with his French friend, the latter had slapped him on the head. "Never do it again," he shouted menacingly. The friend, surprised, retorted that it was a friendly slap. Very angry and very aggressive, the Polynesian explained to him that, throughout his childhood, he had been violently beaten by his parents, by blows to the head. In retrospect, he recognised that if this unfortunate gesture had occurred during a drinking binge, he would have slaughtered his French friend.

Although Arihano's dad always denied it, those around the family had the memory of a violent father and an Arihano, a beaten child.

The hypothesis remains open that a friendly but inappropriate gesture from Stefan on Arihano's head awakened an atavism buried deep in the Marquesan's soul.

The most plausible additional explanation for Arihano's violent slippage is rather to be found in alcohol. Before the arrival of Europeans, Marquesan men were extremely aggressive. They quarrelled, fought and killed each other quite easily. Within the tribes, the extreme codification of social relations and the power of taboos decreed by the tribal chief or the high priest allowed men to mingle and participate in community activities while minimising sources of conflict. On the other hand, the aggressiveness was expressed in the conflicts between the tribes which did not stop fighting and killing each other. The winning fighters ate the defeated fighters.

However, the tribes had to have moments of meeting to settle problems broader than neighbourhood quarrels, for example to ally themselves in order to resist a common enemy or to settle inter-community marriages in order to avoid too much consanguinity. For this purpose, men consumed a natural psychotropic, kava.

This drink was made from a sterile plant that reproduces only by cuttings and whose scientific name is piper methysticum. Its consumption plunged the warriors into such a state of stupor that they managed to discuss among themselves without showing violence or susceptibility. One could not, they said, immediately kill someone with whom one had just shared kava.

The Europeans brought alcohol which was quickly adopted by the Marquesans. They gave up kava. Either way, kava was banned by colonial legislation. While Westerners consume alcohol on a regular basis, albeit in increasing doses over time, the Marquesans retained the method of kava consumption that they had used for centuries. Men gather in groups and massively consume alcohol during the meeting. When the blood alcohol level is low, at the beginning of the meeting, alcohol has the same effects as kava. It's soothing and allows testosterone-heavy men to meet and talk to each other without fighting. As the blood alcohol level increases, the loss of contact with reality increases, but unlike kava, alcohol causes a disinhibition of violence. Alcoholic encounters usually start in good mood and fun and end in a fight.

The cabinets of the Tahiti courthouse are filled with files of serious violence and homicides, between friends or between spouses, occurring on the occasion of excessive alcohol consumption. The perpetrators of these crimes, once sobered up, do not themselves explain how they could have come to this. Wives are frequently abused by their companions who return drunk from these alcoholic gatherings between men. The husband, when he is sobered up, is quite sheepish. Summoned by the gendarmerie, he asks his wife, although she bears the marks of blows, to accompany him "because he does not know what to say". Western judges are disconcerted to see the couple appear in court, husband and wife huddled against each other, mutually protecting each other from the sanction that justice will pronounce against the husband. The wife is sincere when she advocates for her husband and asks for clemency from the courts.

Arihano admitted to the gendarmes that he had drunk to the point of losing all ability to oppose Stefan's advances. At first, the blood alcohol level was at a level that allowed consensual sex between the two men. They continued to drink. Arihano's blood alcohol level soared to a level that caused him to lose touch with reality and disinhibit his male violence. He killed Stefan.

Arihano's improbable tale has a grain of truth. Arihano rewrote the scenario of Stefan's murder by expurgating it of the consented transgression of the taboo of the homosexual act which placed him on the margins of his own society. He turned it into an enforced act under the duress of a weapon, becoming the victim of colonial-like behaviour. This presentation was accepted by his community.

Western justice is not interested in homosexuality, but excuses murder when it is committed in a context of self-defence. Arihano rewrote a script where he was forced to shoot Stefan who threatened to rape him again.

For the sexual assault of Heike, Arihano maintained that he never raped her, that is, he never introduced his sex into Heike's, which is true. Unable to explain in English or German what had happened with Stefan, he had wanted to explain to her what he had suffered from Stefan by reproducing the same scenario on her. The narrative was naive, earning an incredulous shrug from Western judges, but it worked within his community, that was the main thing for him.

8 - EPILOGUE

Until the trial, Arihano was detained in Nuutania. Although this prison is reputed, in the eyes of the International Observatory of Prisons, to be the most dilapidated, the most overcrowded and the most inhuman in all of France, it is not at all perceived in this way by Polynesian prisoners.

Female prisoners are a very small minority and have a separate section. Most of the detainees are men of Polynesian culture, with a low level of education and from a disadvantaged background. They appreciate living together in a cell whose comfort is no worse than that of their home. Often arriving barefoot with just shorts, they appreciate being provided with shorts, underpants, T-shirts and flip-flops, as well as a towel and soap. They appreciate being fed regularly with dishes, certainly not very varied and inexpensive, but more luxurious than those they find at home. They enjoy meeting at regular times, all together, in the prison yard to talk and play. The only things that are really lacking are encounters with women.

The trial took place two and a half years after the events, before the Assise Court of Papeete, composed of three judges and six jurors, drawn by lot from the electoral lists. His lawyer told reporters: "You have to be realistic. French criminal procedure is a prosecution procedure. It is a constant fact. All you have to do is read the order for referral to the Assise Court. To support that Arihano is a liar, the order lists the points on which he allegedly lied, but does not retain the hearings which say the opposite. It chooses voluntarily to darken his personality to let the jurors think that he is a liar, that he is violent... The prosecutor presents him as a monster, while many hearings are concordant to say that he is someone kind, helpful, certainly lonely, but who, whenever he could help, did so without counterpart and that, when they recognise that he can be violent, all without exception specify that it is when assaulted and never the first.

"The sentence you give me, I will accept it", declared in Marquesan the accused, at the end of the trial and when the court was about to retire to deliberate. "I did kill Stefan and for his wife, I regret what I did to her. I would like to bow down to Stefan's father and mother because I recognize their pain; but for Stefan, I'm not going to say sorry to him just yet. I will wait for the condemnation and I will make prayers to him."

On 16 May 2014, the Assize Court, after six hours of deliberation, found Arihano guilty of the murder on 9 October 2011 of German tourist Stefan and guilty of the sexual assault at gunpoint and the confinement of Heike, his companion.

On May 16, 2014, the Assise Court, after six hours of deliberation, found Arihano guilty of the October 9, 2011 murder of German tourist Stefan and guilty of sexual assault at gunpoint and kidnapping of Heike, his companion.

He was sentenced to 28 years' imprisonment, including 18 years of security. For 18 years, Arihano will not be able to benefit from any adjustment to his detention, such as a semi-freedom regime or conditional release. He will not be released before the age of 49, given the two years of preventive detention he served between his arrest and his trial.

Arihano did not appeal his conviction. The verdict was accepted by his family. When the sentence was announced, his father cried out. "The Lord has heard my prayer; my child will not be in prison all his life".

The first five years of his detention following his conviction took place in mainland France, first of all, in the famous prison of Fleury-Mérogis, located near Paris. It is the largest prison in Europe which accommodates 3,600 prisoners and has 1,300 guards. On paper, prison conditions are more acceptable than Nuutania's for long-term prisoners. In reality, it is a high place of violence and suicides. Arihano frequented a population of mafiosos and religious fanatics whose culture, codes and behaviours are absolutely foreign to his Marquesan universe.

Arihano did not find the friendliness of Nuutania as evidenced by the small additional sentence he suffered before his departure to Fleury-Mérogis. He had been caught in possession of a glass pipette and pakalolo, the Polynesian name for cannabis, during the period of incarceration in Nuutania pending his trial before the Assises. He had been sentenced to an additional one month in prison for drug use in prison.

After Fleury-Mérogis, Arihano found himself in the penitentiary on Ré Island, of a more modest size. This prison is located inside the fortifications built in the 17th century to protect the inhabitants. In the 19th century, the fortified citadel was used to bring together prisoners condemned to forced labour from all over France before sending them to the penal colony of Cayenne in South America or to that of New Caledonia in the Pacific. It is from this high historical and symbolic place that Arihano will return to Tahiti.

The European Court of Human Rights has condemned France for inhuman and degrading conditions in its prison establishments, which has opened, since 2012, remedies for compensation on the part of prisoners. These appeals are supervised by the International Observatory of Prisons.

Compensation claims claim that with an occupancy rate of 327.8% as of May 1, 2016, Nuutania prison is the most overcrowded prison establishment in France. The detainees are crammed into 3 or 4 cells in 9 m2 cells with dirty walls and covered with mould, without drinking water or hot water. The toilets are not partitioned off, guaranteeing no privacy. There is a foul smell due to the under-sizing of the treatment plant and the lack of aeration device in the cells. Insects, rats and mice proliferate. Overcrowding makes it impossible to guarantee the separation between defendants and convicts, between minors and adults, between smokers and non-smokers. Access to care is lacking, the number of caregivers being determined by the theoretical capacity of the establishment. In 2012, only a hundred out of 400 prisoners had access to a weekly activity.

Like all his fellow prisoners, Arihano asked the administrative court to be compensated for the two years, from November 30, 2011 to October 22, 2013, that he served in Nuutania. A compensation scale of €4 per day of detention is usually applied.

While he was incarcerated in France, the French state, harassed by non-governmental organisations and European authorities, built a model prison on the island of Tahiti, called Tatutu, after the land on which it was built. The Tatutu prison was inaugurated in March 2017 and Arihano was transferred there in December 2017. This is where he will finish serving his sentence.

THE END